My Art Workbook

An Interactive Guide of Tips, Techniques and Exercises to Help you Learn To Draw

Featuring
Jon Gnagy

By

Brad L. Johnson

Copyright © 2014 Brad L Johnson

All rights reserved.

ISBN:
ISBN-13: **978-1493732906**
ADDITIONAL WORKS BY THE AUTHOR
Tynk ! of Neverland
Bits & Pieces Vol 1
TYNK ! (The Movie Version)
Tynk ! For Young Readers (The Movie Version)
The Slightly Whacked Vegetarian Cookbook For Regular People
The Comic Collectors Handbook Vol 1
Peace Corp Frebon (the Comic Book)

Online with Writer Brad L. Johnson
www.bradljohnson.webs.com

DEDICATION

This book is for all the undiscovered artists.
This book is for all the artists who draw only for themselves.
This book is for all the artists who do not yet know they are artists.

CONTENTS

	Acknowledgments	i
1	Why Are We Here ?	1
2	How To Use This Workbook	6
3	Shape of Things to Come	7
4	Old School 3-D	13
5	Cast a Shadow	17
6	Get Some Perspective	23
7	Cross Hatching	33
8	Outlining	49
9	Tracing	53
10	Fun Stuff	74

ACKNOWLEDGMENTS

Beyond the obvious....after all, this book would not exist without Jon Gnagy, thanks to Polly Gnagy Seymour and Thaddeus Seymour for keeping Jon's legacy alive on-line. Thanks also to Bob Smith at the Idyllwild Museum.

www.ircpage.org/Jon_Gnagy_Art/Jon_Gnagy_Home.html

To Youtube for giving Jon a new forum.

GO TO YOUTUBE AND SEARCH JON GNAGY FOR 13+ VIDEO LESSONS

1. WHY ARE WE HERE ?

Jon Gnagy changed lives. If you were like me, and millions of other kids, you spent a boatload of Saturdays or Sundays hunkered down in front of your TV with a #2 pencil and a few sheets of paper. My brother Bill and I would faithfully watch Jon and learned how to draw anything using his simple but effective techniques utilizing the sphere, cylinder, cube and cone. My brother went on to become a great artist. I was not that good.... so I became a writer. Even so, Jon inspired me and nurtured a love for sketching that continues to this day. My introduction to art by Jon led me on a life long journey that has taken me to art galleries all across America , England, Wales and Scotland. They attract me like a magnet. I even opened and ran an Artist Village in Northern California and am now on the Board of Directors of El Morro Area Arts Council. We are not alone. Many of those who watched his show, the first of it's kind, became artists, including Andy Warhol who said, "Jon Gnagy taught me how to draw." Some became teachers and used his techniques to teach the next generation of artists. Many passed their love for Jon's lessons to their children and grandchildren. Many more proclaim that because of Jon and his show, art was introduced to their young lives and enriched it. Louis Fontana remembers Jon:

" I USED TO WATCH JON GNAGY AS A CHILD ON TV. HE WAS A MAN THAT , IF YOU HAD A DREAM OR TALENT FOR ART, HE WAS THE ONE YOU TURNED TO. YOU

 LEARNED FROM A MASTER OF ART.... WHO TOOK THE TIME TO SHOW YOU WHAT YOU NEEDED TO KNOW. HE WAS A CALM, PEACEFUL MAN WITH SUCH A TALENT. A TRUE ARTIST OF HIS DAY."

Here is a sketch Jon did that Mr. Fontana sent us.

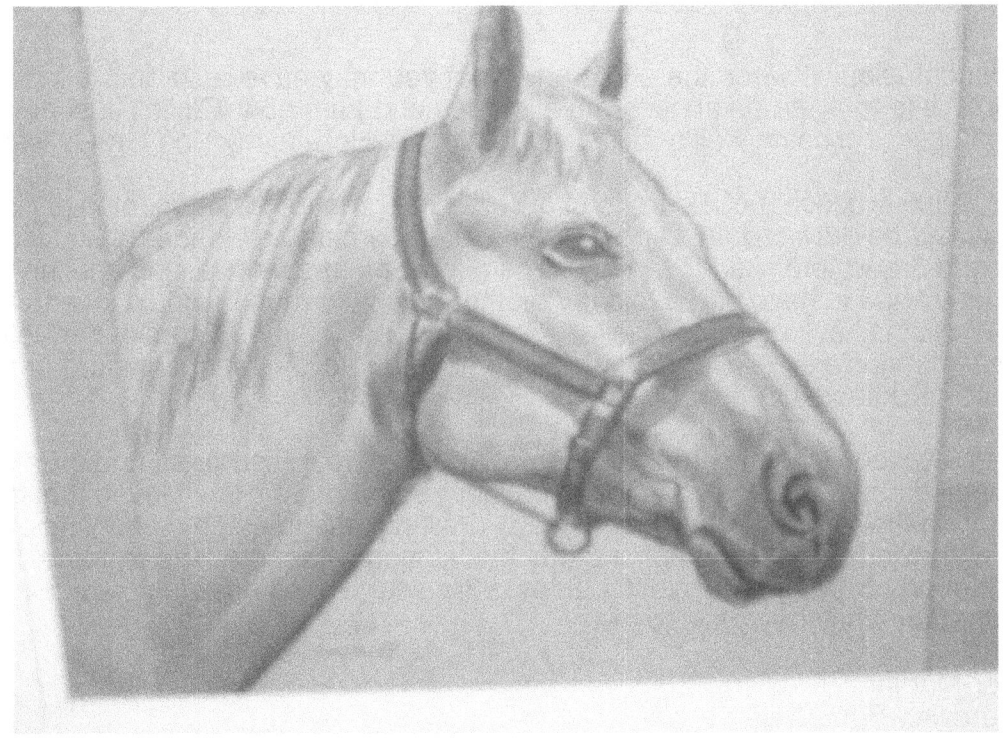

We received this wonderful photo and email from Olivia Snyder-Martinez:

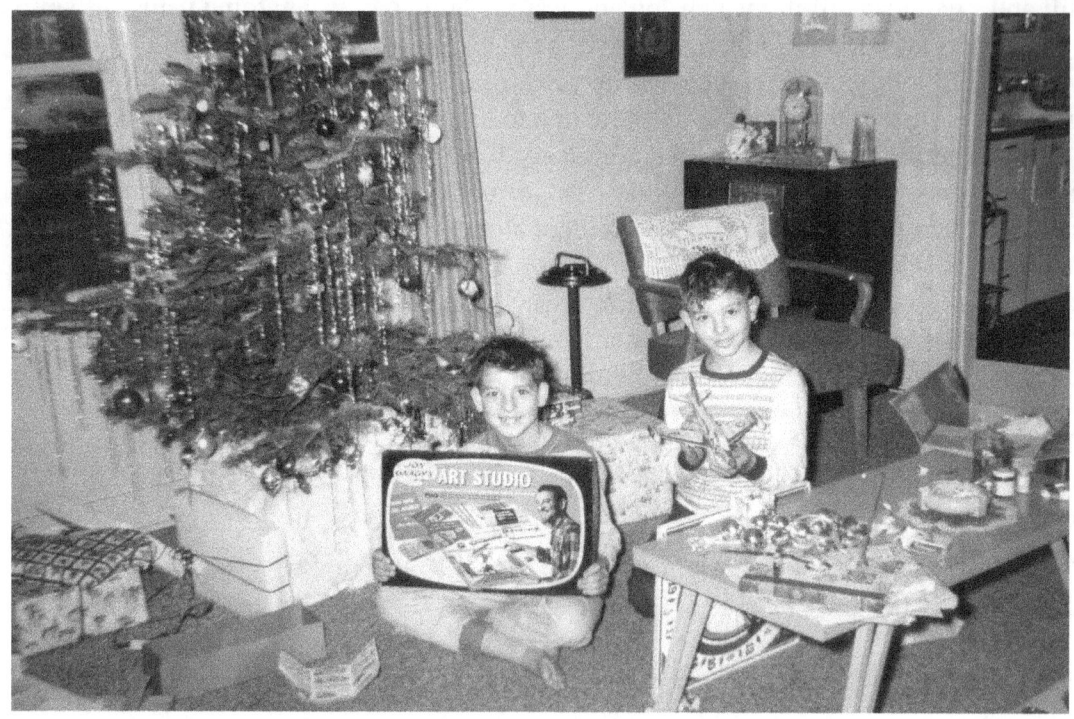

To avoid any confusion between the photo and what you may have read, this is indeed me in the mid 1950's. Life took me on an incredible journey and I am now 'Olivia'. Just didn't want you to be confused. I'm doing well and life is good to me. Here is my 'Jon Gnagy' story..............

I would await each broadcast of 'Learn to Draw' with the greatest excitement in my young mind. What would he draw today? I knew I would learn something wonderful and looked forward to trying to draw more like Mr. Gnagy. When I saw the drawing lesson sets he would show us, I knew I had to have one. I told my mother how very much I would love to have a Jon Gnagy set. We didn't have access in Dallas, Oregon for such things. Mom in her determination to make my Christmas a special one, was able to have our local stationary store order the set from J. K. Gill in Portland, Oregon.

Well, the long awaited Christmas morning came, and what to my surprise and great joy and so carefully wrapped under the tree, was the thing I longed for most. How I loved that gift. Watching Mr. Gnagy on the television and with my new drawing lesson set, my imagination could come alive in drawings. That is something that has stayed with me all these years, having given me a love of art, drawing and painting. In my 63rd year, I'm so grateful to Jon Gnagy and my dear mother for what they gave to me.

Olivia Snyder-Martinez
And then there is ...Bob.

R.T. Crowley is President of the Apex Art Council in North Carolina, he wrote:

"I remember John Gnagy well, Brad. He was my first real introduction to the whole world of art when I was a very small child. I remember watching his TV show every week and bugging my grandfather to include a stop at Art Brown and Brothers in trips into New York City. In the end, I found I could not draw or paint to save my life, settling on writing as my art form, but watching him inspired me to haunt the great museums around the world, adding much to my education and appreciation for art and the world beyond."

Right before we went to print, I heard from Margerat Moschell, an art instructor from Mason, Ohio. Here is her story and picture.

"I have vivid memories of being 5 years old in Middletown, Ohio, and watching Jon Gnagy on T.V. Of course, color TV had not been invented, which was probably why he worked in charcoal and grey chalks. Hearing "The Artisit's Life" would alert me that his show was on and I would sit mesmerized as I watched the magic of his drawings unfold. I decided I wanted to be an artist, just like Jon. My Kindergarten classroom had easels and paint and I spent many happy hours there. Mrs. Jones showed my mother a painting I made of a rural mailbox over and over, with snowmen in the background and dots of snow in the air, and no one could figure out where it came from, because in my neighborhood, our mailboxes where attached to the house next to our front doors. Mom taped my painting to the door of the basement in our dining room, and to the walls as well. I loved the attention from my teacher and parents for my artistic talent, and as I grew up my art teachers and classroom teaches also gave me a lot of praise and confidence.

When I was 11, Mom and I were in an art supply store and I discovered Jon's Learn to Draw kit. I begged her to buy it, even thought I know it was probably too expensive. To my utter delight, she bought it and I remember promising her with all my heart that this investment would pay off because I would become an artisit. I spent hours with the kit, and later when I was studying Art Education at the University of Concinnati, I bought another kit because my old book was falling apart. As a future art teacher, I wanted to learn Jon's techniqures for convincing even a 5 year old that I could make beautiful art, step by simple step, and practice.

I still share my Learn to Draw book with my fourth grade art students. They are just as impressed as I am with Jon's step by step instructions and shading techiques. I still have my original blending stomp, which was like a magic wand years ago. I play music in my art room while my students work, so of course I play "An Artists Life" beccause I know that many of my students are taking their first steps toward becoming artists, and I want to use all of Jon's magic to help them believe in themselves enought to struggle through practicing drawing techiques. Every now and then, I still hear the exact version of the song from Jon's show, and it never fails to make my heart skip a beat.

I haven't drawn a "Gnagy drawing" in years, so it was a joy to revisit the snowy scene that thrilled me so long ago--although I clearly rememeber icicles under the mailbox, so I used "artisitic license" and added them to my drawing. I added a set of footprints in the snow, imagining that those are my footsteps and Jon is next to me."

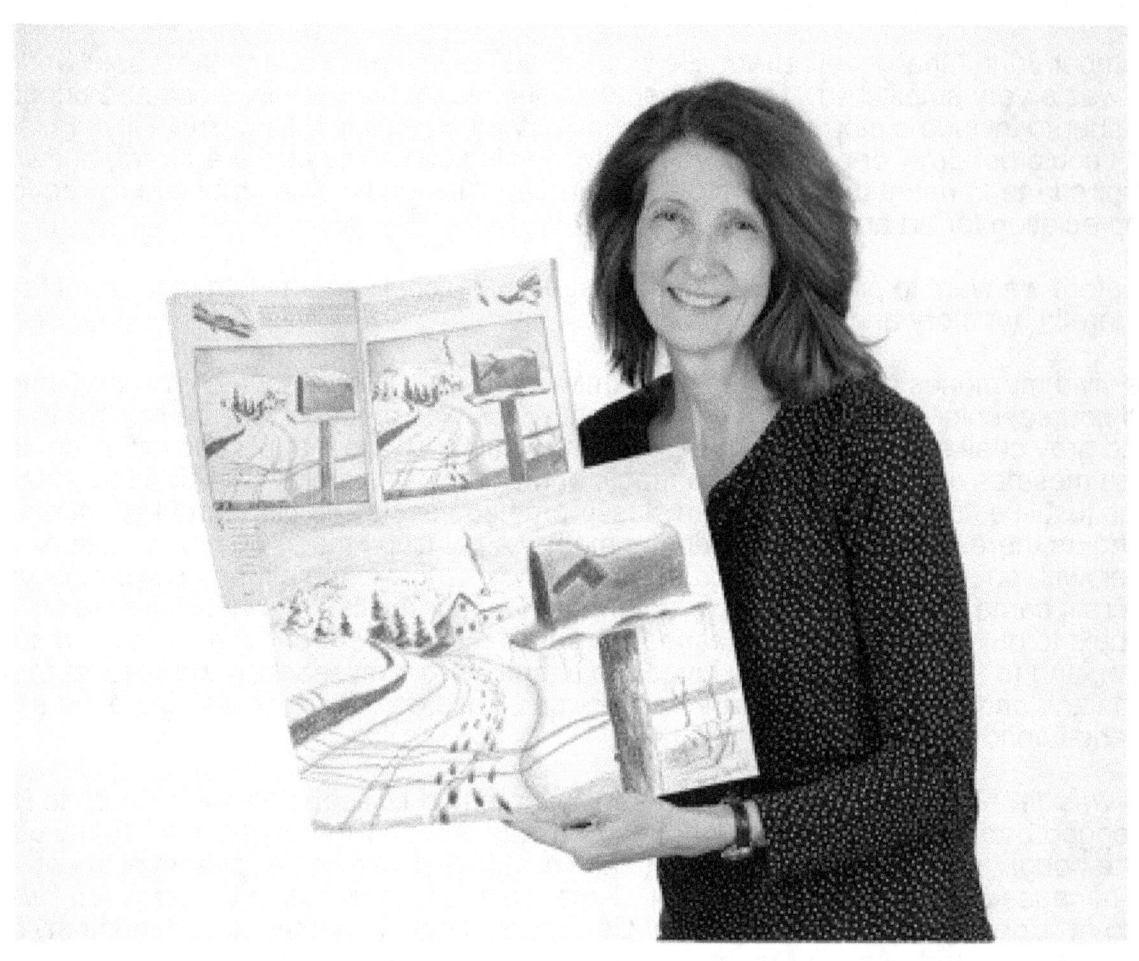

There are many more stories and reminisces like this on the Official Jon Gnagy Website along with lessons, articles, bio, and his fine art. I encourage you to go there and poke around.

We want to extend our heartfelt thanks to Polly Gnagy Seymor and Thaddeus Seymor for being so gracious and available.

Before we get into how to use this workbook I wanted to share some quick facts about Jon Gnagy:

- ✓ He was the first art instructor on TV (starting in 1946 when NBC broadcast it's first show from a brand new antennae on the Empire State Building)
- ✓ His drawing kits have sold in excess of 15 million copies (and that was as of 1986 !)

- ✓ During World War II, Jon taught camouflage techniques.
- ✓ His show "Learn to Draw" went out of syndication in 1970. At that time it was the longest running show on TV.
- ✓ At its height, his show had 60 million viewers.

"I believe that you have an un-explored talent. My conviction grows stronger every year as I find thousands of people just like you searching to express something"   -Jon Gnagy

2. HOW TO USE THIS WORKBOOK

We have put together this interactive guide to help you explore your drawing abilities in an easy, fun and organic way. I was taught my first art lessons by Jon. I felt, while writing this book, that I should draw some of the illustrations myself, after all, I am not an artist but I have incorporated many of the tips and techniques Jon was famous for....but with a twist. Nothing will ever compare with the original Learn to Draw book that Jon wrote in 1950.
Do not feel like you have to start at the beginning and follow it to the end....jump around, try out what you feel like drawing that day. If you don't like our suggestion for the page you are on....DRAW SOMETHING ELSE....BUT DRAW. By the way, even though there is plenty of room to draw in your guide, we would suggest you get a sketch pad because, well face it...there is never enough when you really get going.
Ok...here's what you need plus some other optional cool stuff to have:

A PENCIL.
Any pencil will do, of course, but if you get your hands on a CARBON PENCIL you will have a lot more fun.
AN ERASER.
It will help you take out what you don't want to see until you are better. And let's face it, we ALL make mistakes !

There are a few other really amazing tools you can get like :

CHALK ...Jon's kit came with three. Light gray, Dark Gray and Black.
A piece of **SANDPAPER** to change the tip of your pencil from rounded to chisel.
A STOMP. This is a a rolled up piece of soft paper that looks like a pencil. you can use it with chalk for shading.
TISSUE. To help you do soft blends on paper.

Here is a photo of what came with Jon's kit.

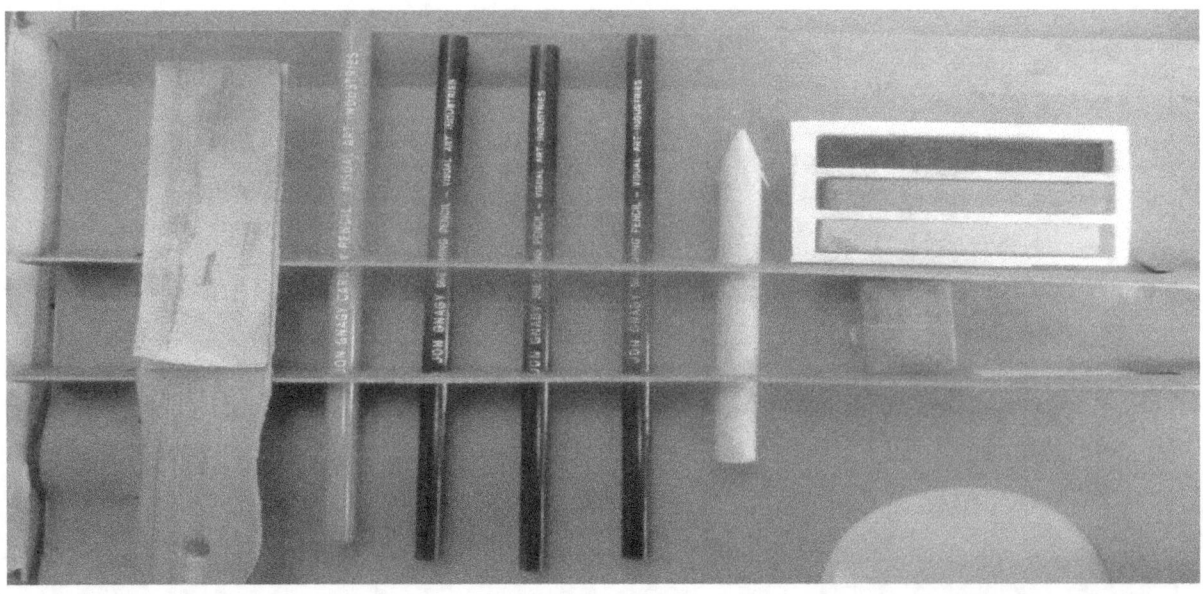

3. THE SHAPE OF THINGS TO COME: CUBE, SPHERE, CONE & CYLINDER
(OTHERWISE KNOWN AS SQUARE, CIRCLE, TRIANGLE AND RECTANGLE)

A lot of what you draw will be variations of these four shapes. Jon Gnagy based almost everything he taught on these. It is a classic method used by artists Caravaggio, Cezanne and was extolled by Socrates and the ancient Egyptians. It was not new, but television was and Jon used this medium to inspire and instruct. So let's start where Jon did. On the next few pages draw circles, squares, triangles and rectangles of a few different sizes. We will return to these with a fun exercise later after we work on making them three diminsional and shading them.

Shapes

Circle

Square

Triangle

4. OLD SCHOOL 3-D

Practise turning your shapes into 3-D objects. Try drawing them from different angles. Use a stack of books or a soda can or a ball if that helps. Walk around them and over them to change your perspective.

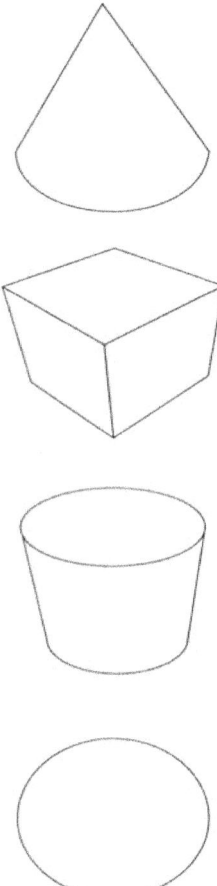

5. CAST A SHADOW

The use of light is critical in learning to draw. Decide where your light is shining from and practise "lighting" your 3-D drawings. If it helps, use a lamp to "light" your way.

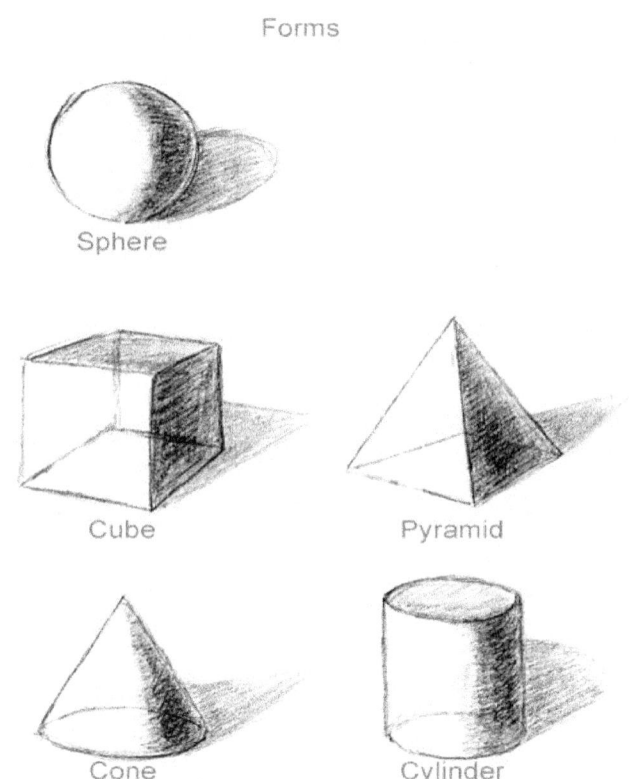

6. GET SOME PERSPECTIVE !

Don't let this part throw you. It is a bit technical but can be fun. The two issues are "eye level" or "horizon" and "vanishing point". Check out the drawing below and try your hand with the following exercises. The vanishing point can be anywhere but all share the same "eye level". Here are some examples and diagrams. On the following pages draw your eye level then experiment with different shapes and vanishing points. Just use basic shapes for now and return to this exercise and you can turn your shapes into "real" objects.

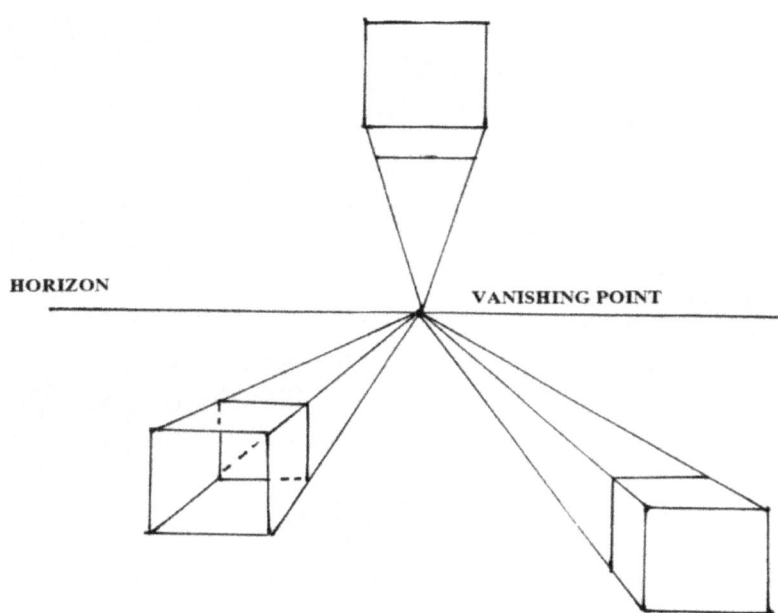

Try this simple drawing using perspective.

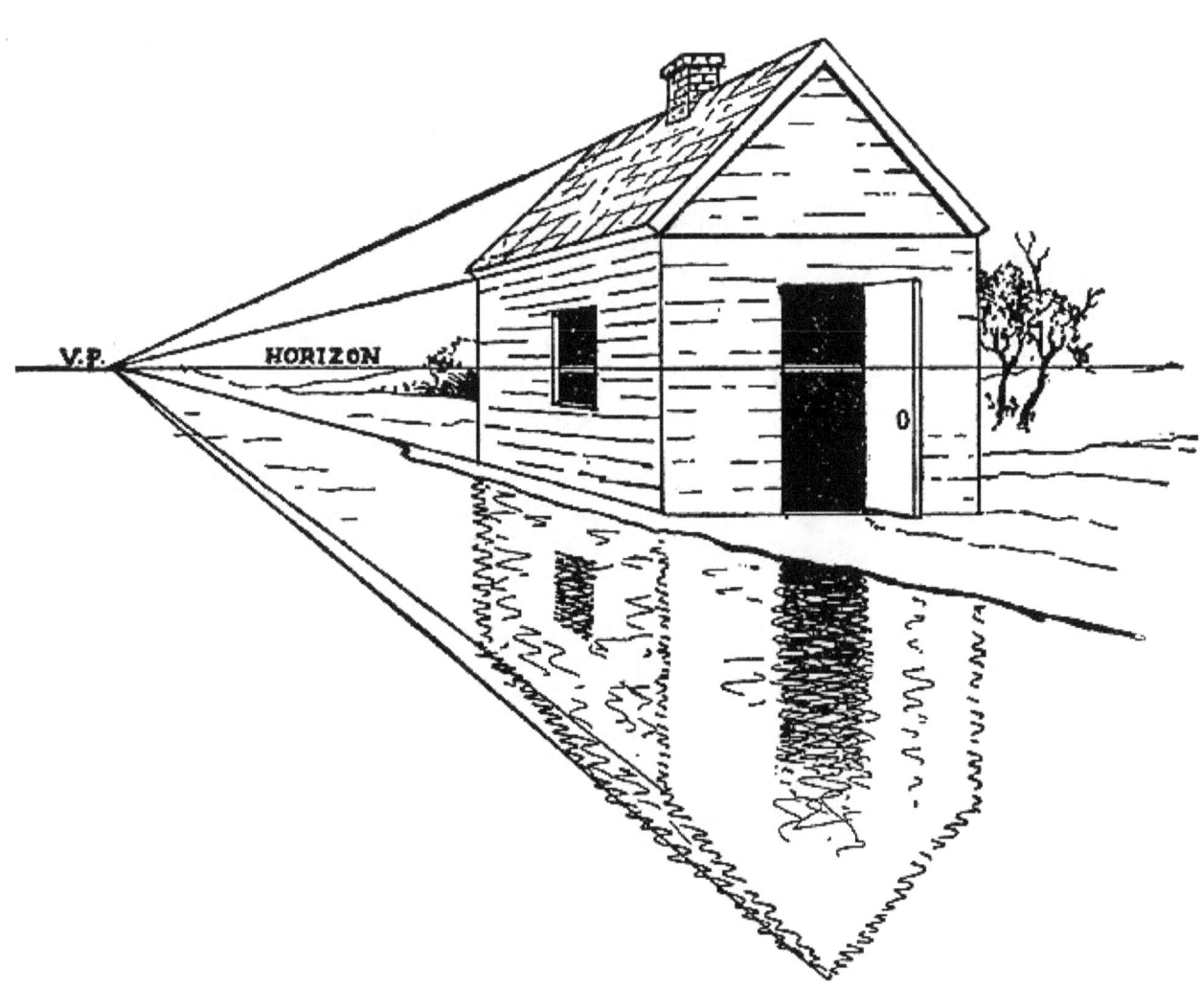

7. CROSS-HATCHING

Cross hatching is a technique used by the artist to give form, substance and shading to their drawings. They say "the devil is in the details" and using this technique can improve your drawings immensely. Have fun ! Start by trying your hand at the different styles. Remember, you can follow the contour of a line with any type of cross hatching adding depth and creativity to your picture...even a stick figure ! Start with the simplest ones and get comfortable with doing it then follow the examples on the next few pages all the way to the example of a dramatic drawing done entirely with cross hatching. There is no right or wrong with this technique just different results...whether your lines are perfectly spaced or all over the place. Remember...use your inner eye...draw what you see (or don't see). Here are some examples of cross hatching try them all or make up your own:

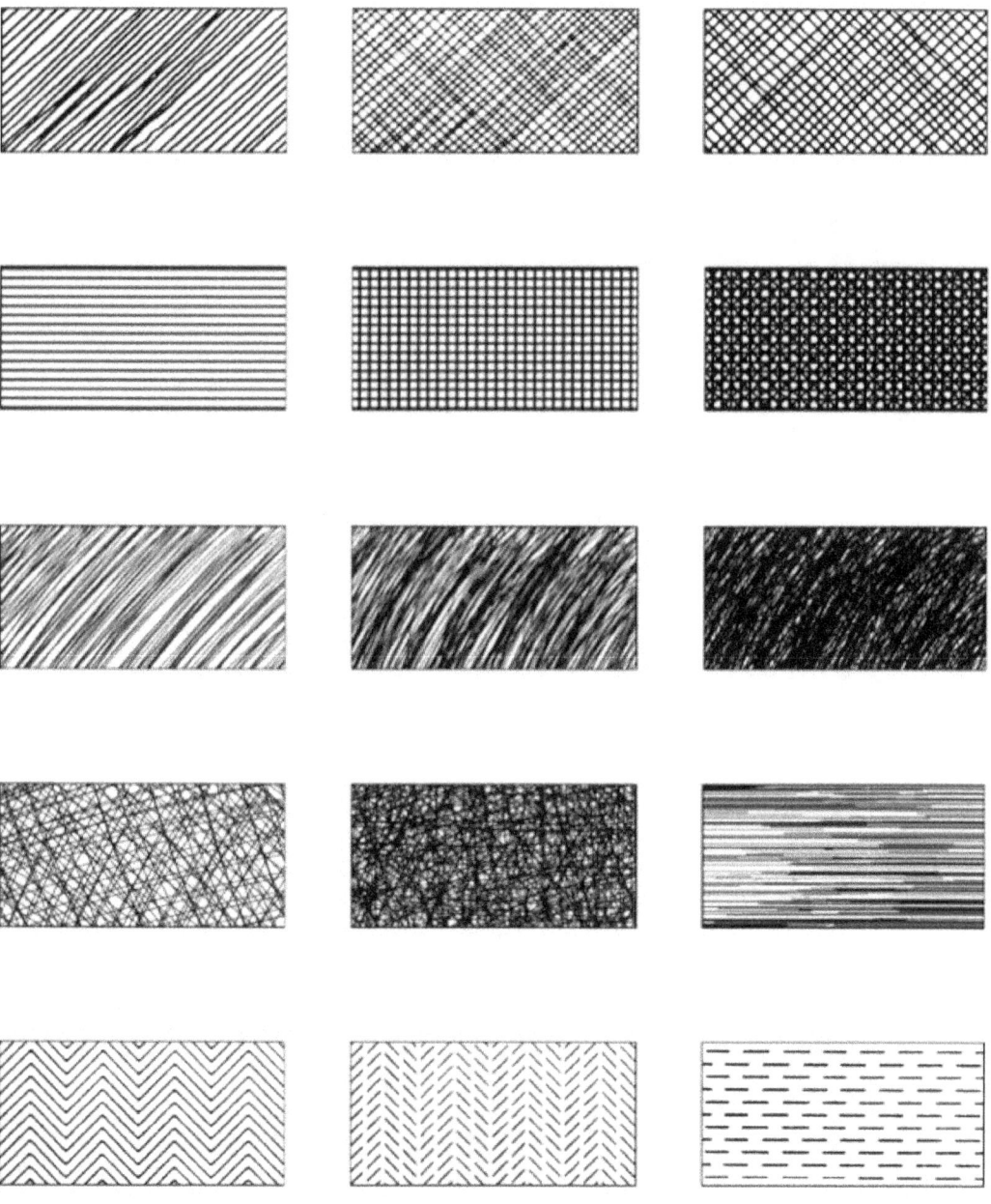

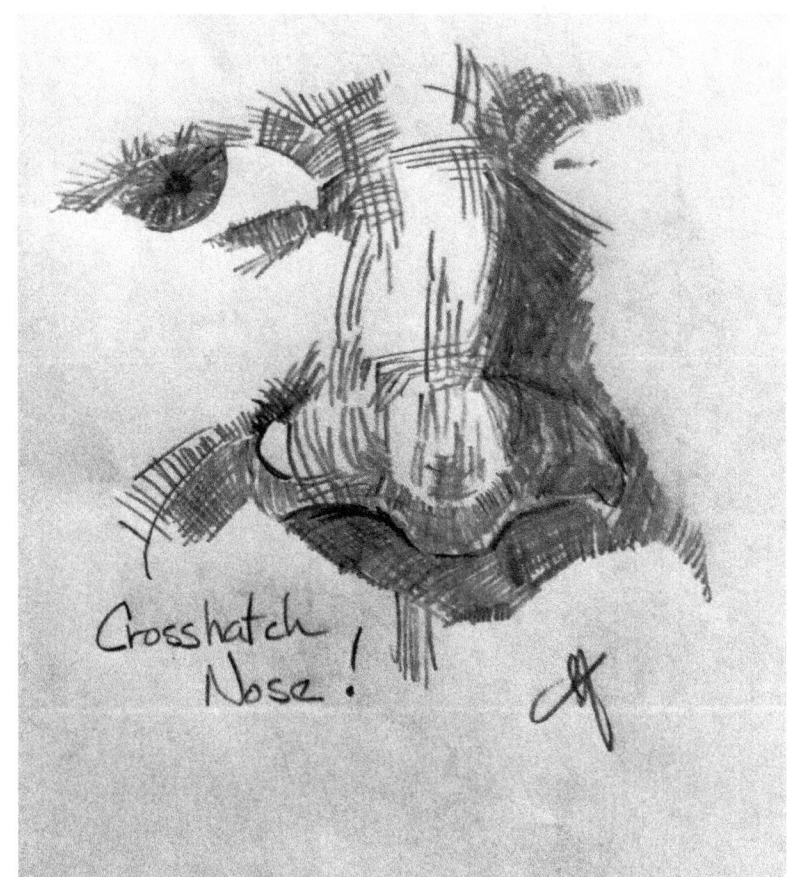

HERE IS A CROSS HATCH NOSE I DID...TRY IT !
THEN TRY THE GLASS AND PUMPKIN.

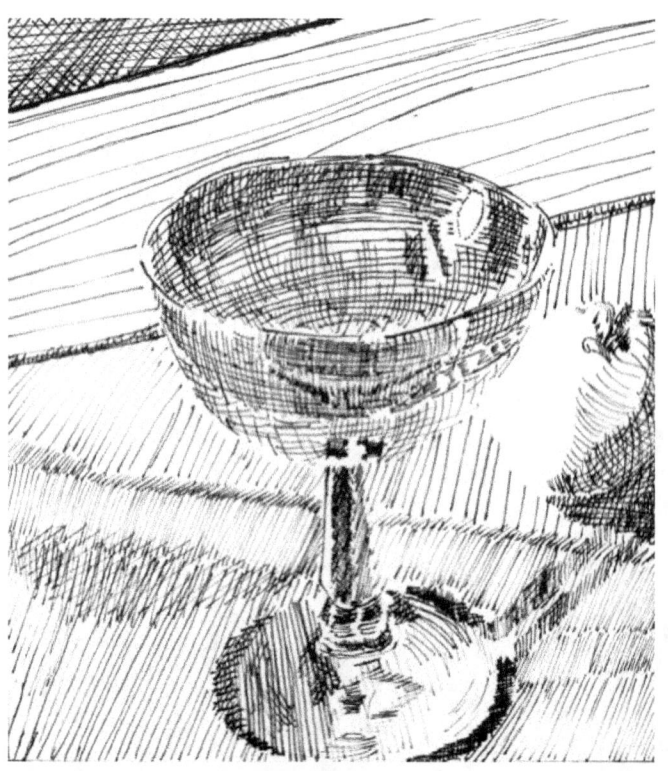

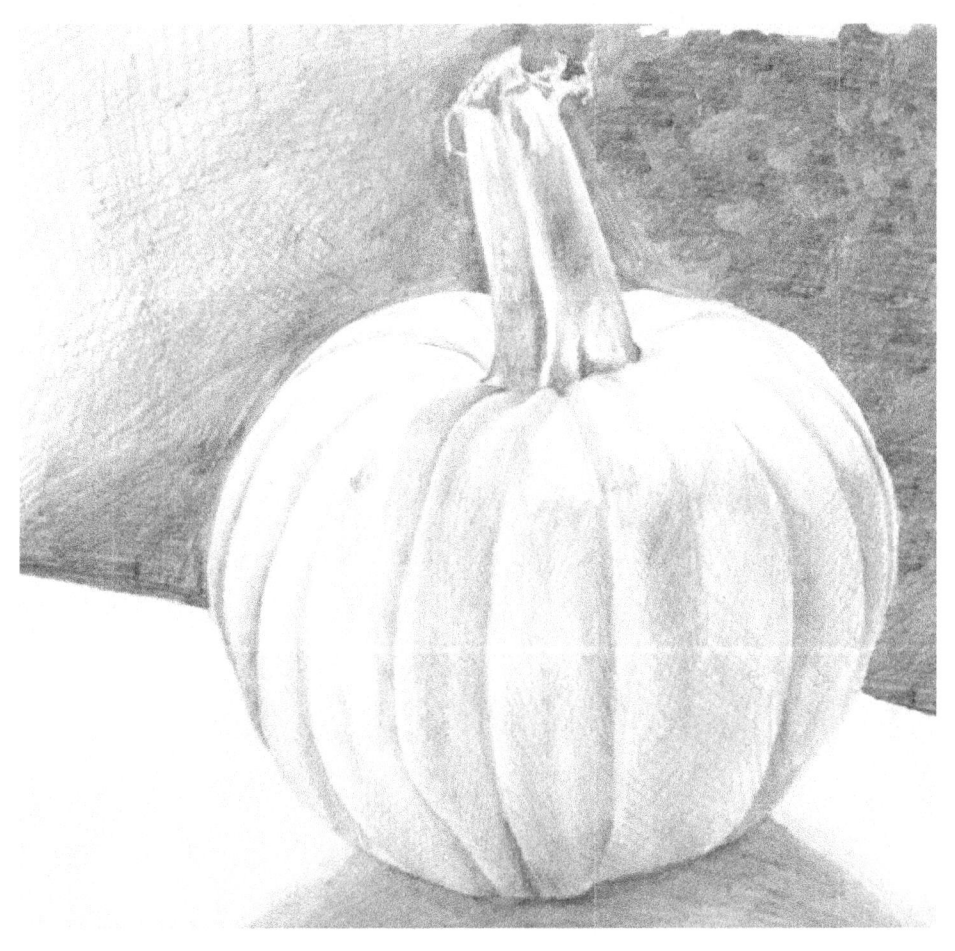

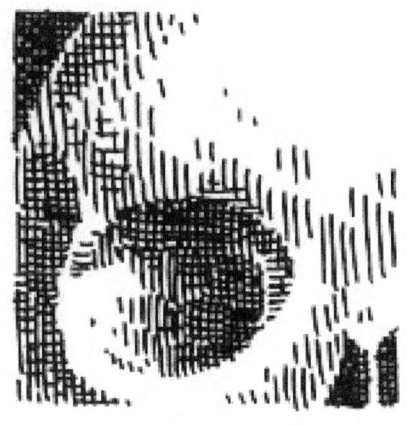 STRAIGHT

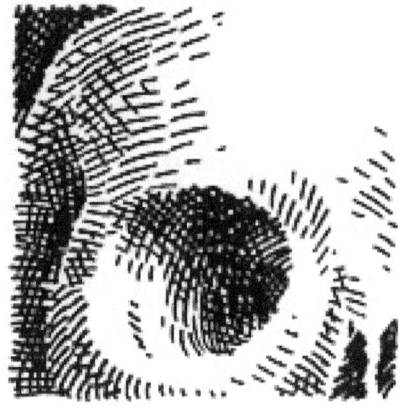 CONTOUR

8. OUTLINING

Outlining a shaded or cross hatched drawing lends an air of distinction to some drawings. Later on we will give you an exercise to explore this technique. You can use outlining to make a drawing look more "cartoony" or give substance to your newly developed cross-hatching technique. Here is a great example of how outling can enhance your drawing by Michael from Australia. On the next page I have drawn a tree using cross hatching. On one of them, outline the tree and see how it changes the drawing. Feel free to add additional lines to make the bark look more realistic. Then draw something simple and whimsical on the next pages using cross hatching, then outline it with a darker pencil mark.

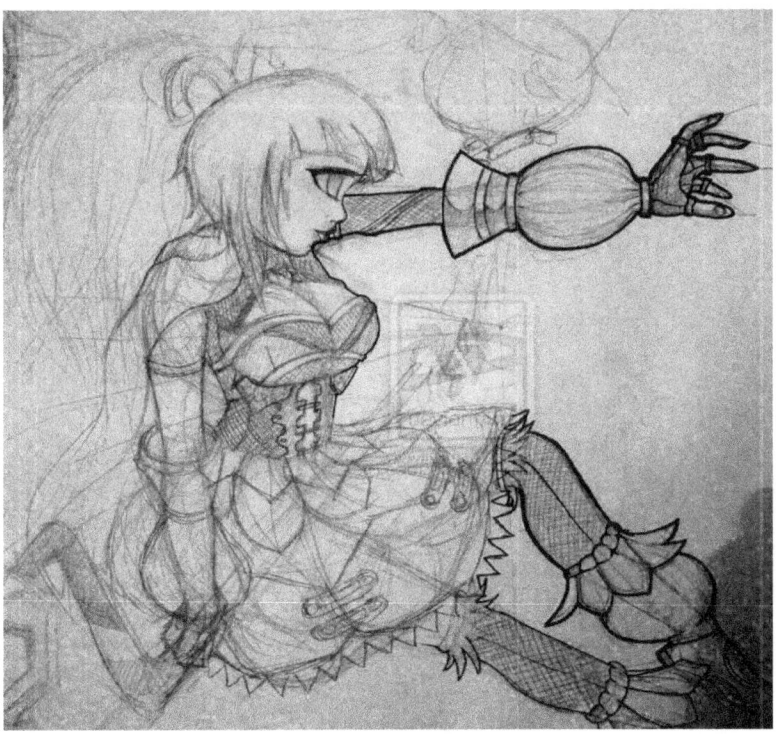

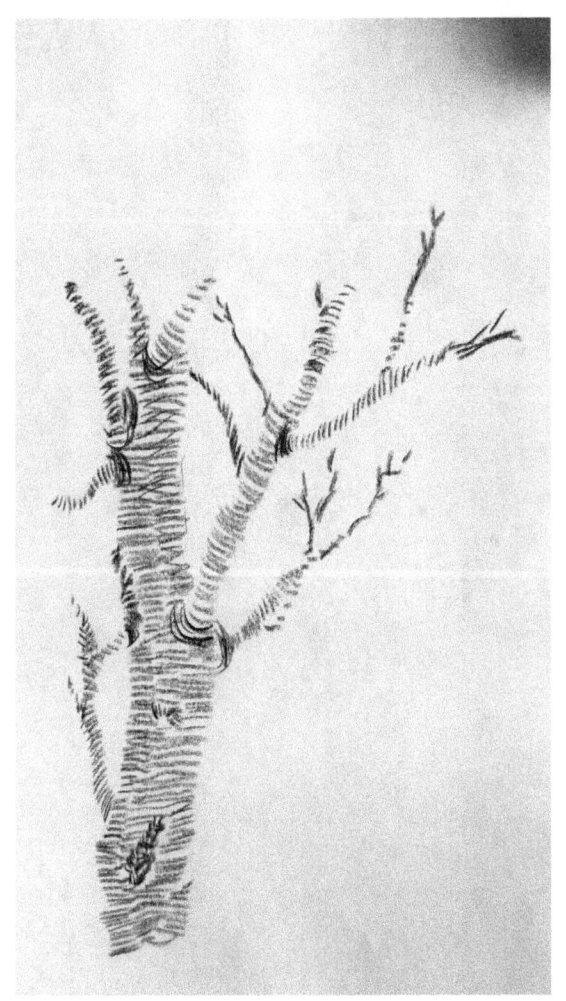 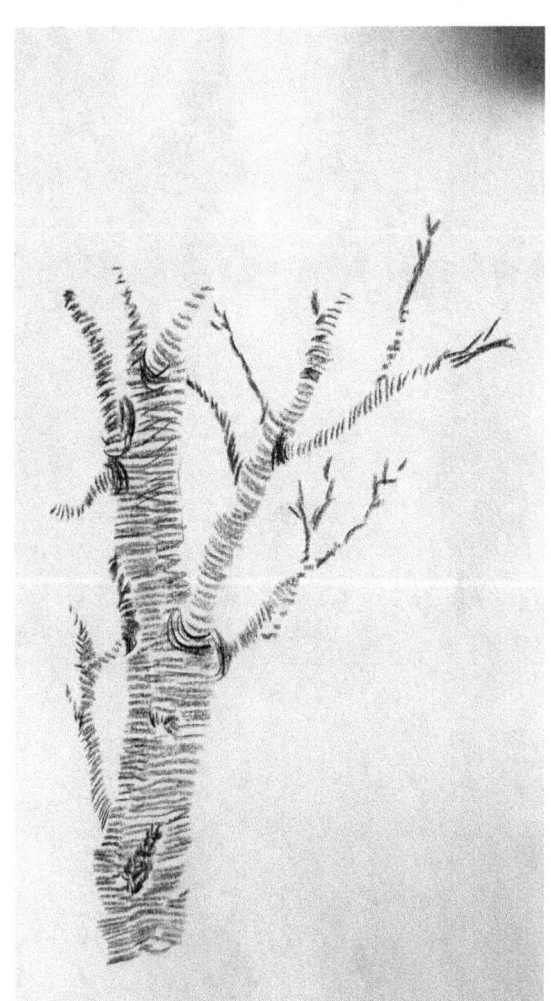

9. TRACING

Tracing a picture or drawing has gotten a "bad rap" but many artists use it (although they won't admit it). Tracing can be used to enhance a drawing especially if you use it carefully and add your own element of creativity. Below is a picture of Jon Gnagy I drew from a photograph using tracing, cross-hatching and creativity. the first image is a quick tracing of the basic look. I then added bits and pieces, in layers until I arrived at my own unique drawing. Although it resembles the photo I used it is my own original tribute.This is great to make gifts for your friends and family. Many artists use a "light box". In it's simplest form it is a wooden box with a plexiglass top with a light (preferably flourescent) under it. I have used a glass coffee table or a piece of glass from an 8x10 photo frame, held up by books on each side and a small lamp underneath....still works. It allows light to come up through what you are drawing and all you have to do is place a blank piece of paper on top. At the end of this chapter is a quick DIY guide to making a light box for as little as $20 with a Tupperware container, Tap lights and batteries.
Here is the basic Jon Gnagy tracing followed by a series of pics showing my addition of cross hatching and dark lines, I urge you to go trace a photo of someone you know and try this :

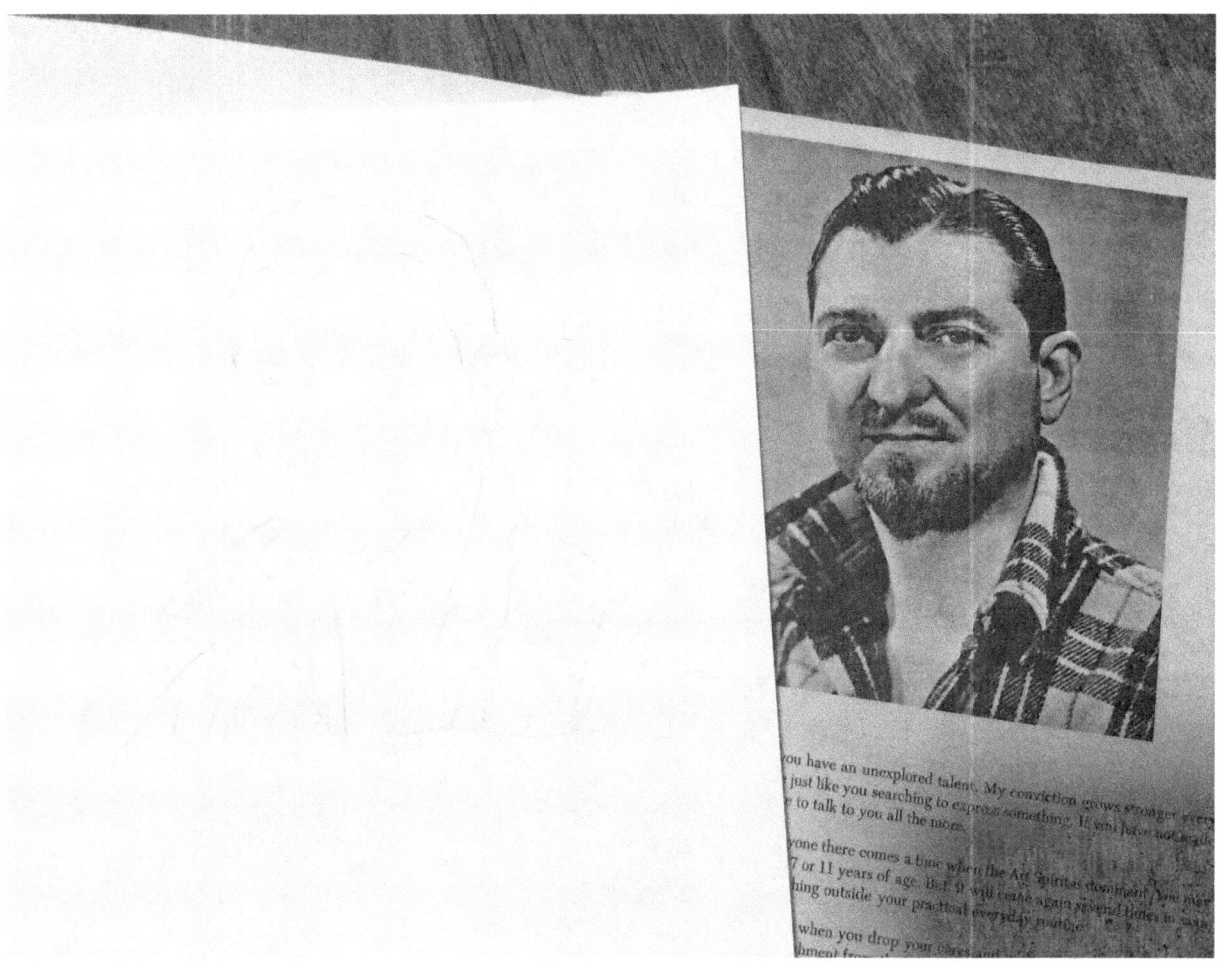

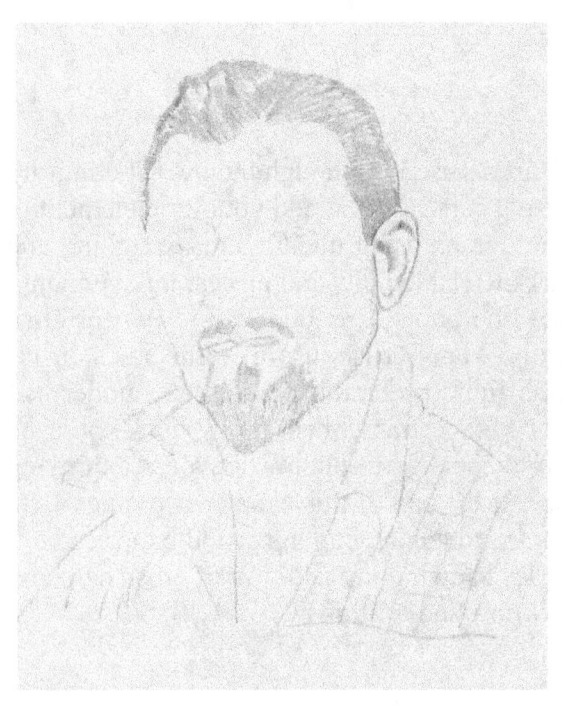
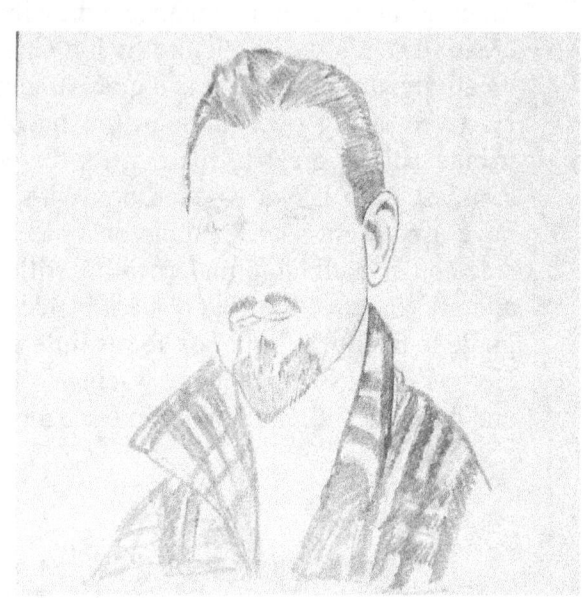
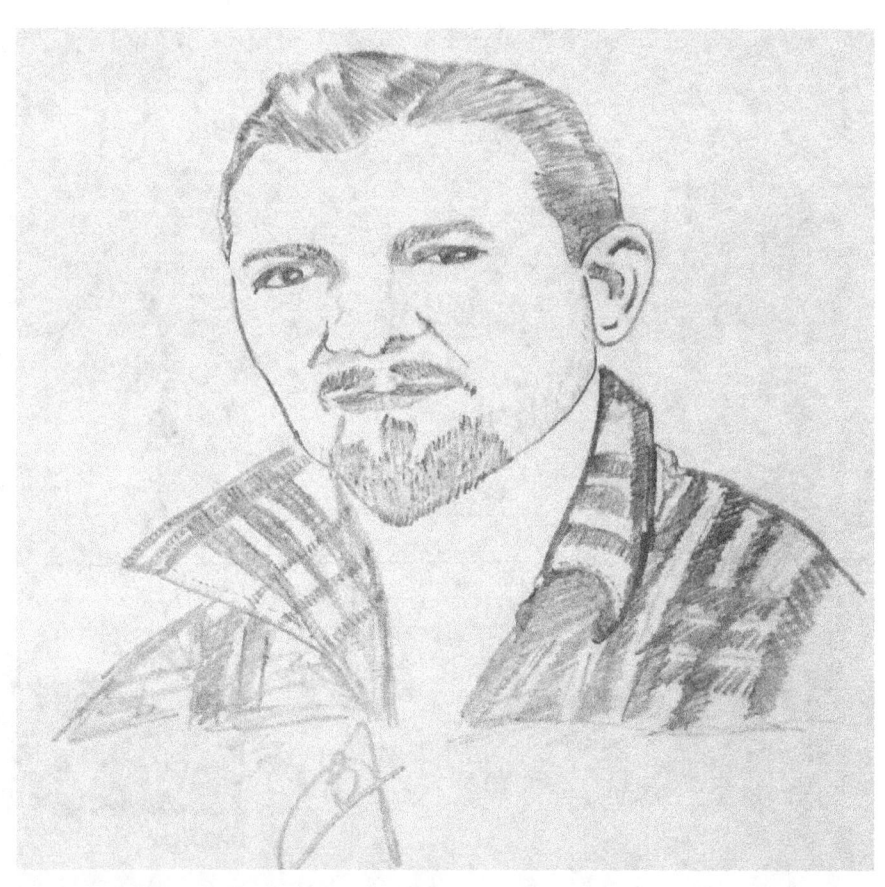

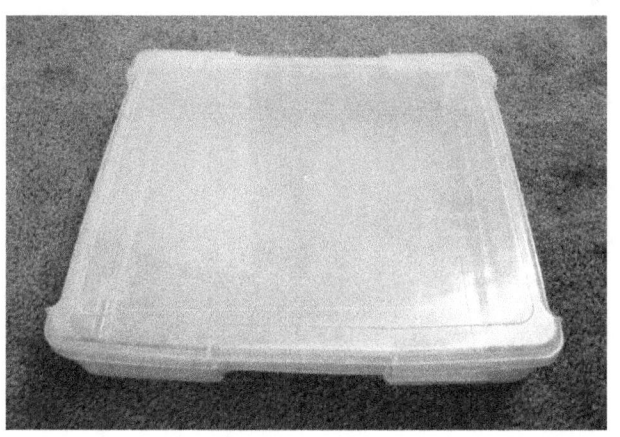
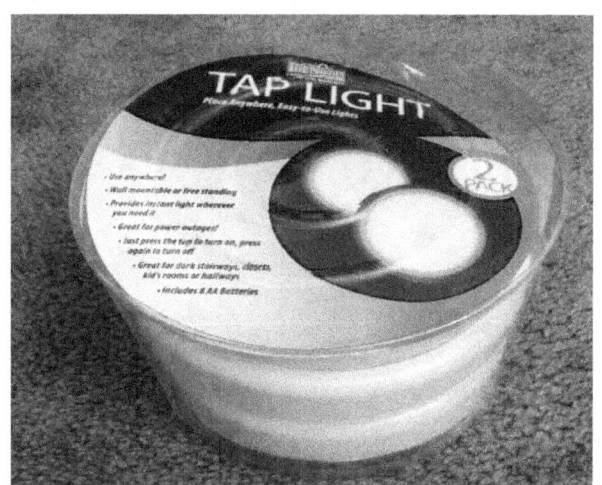

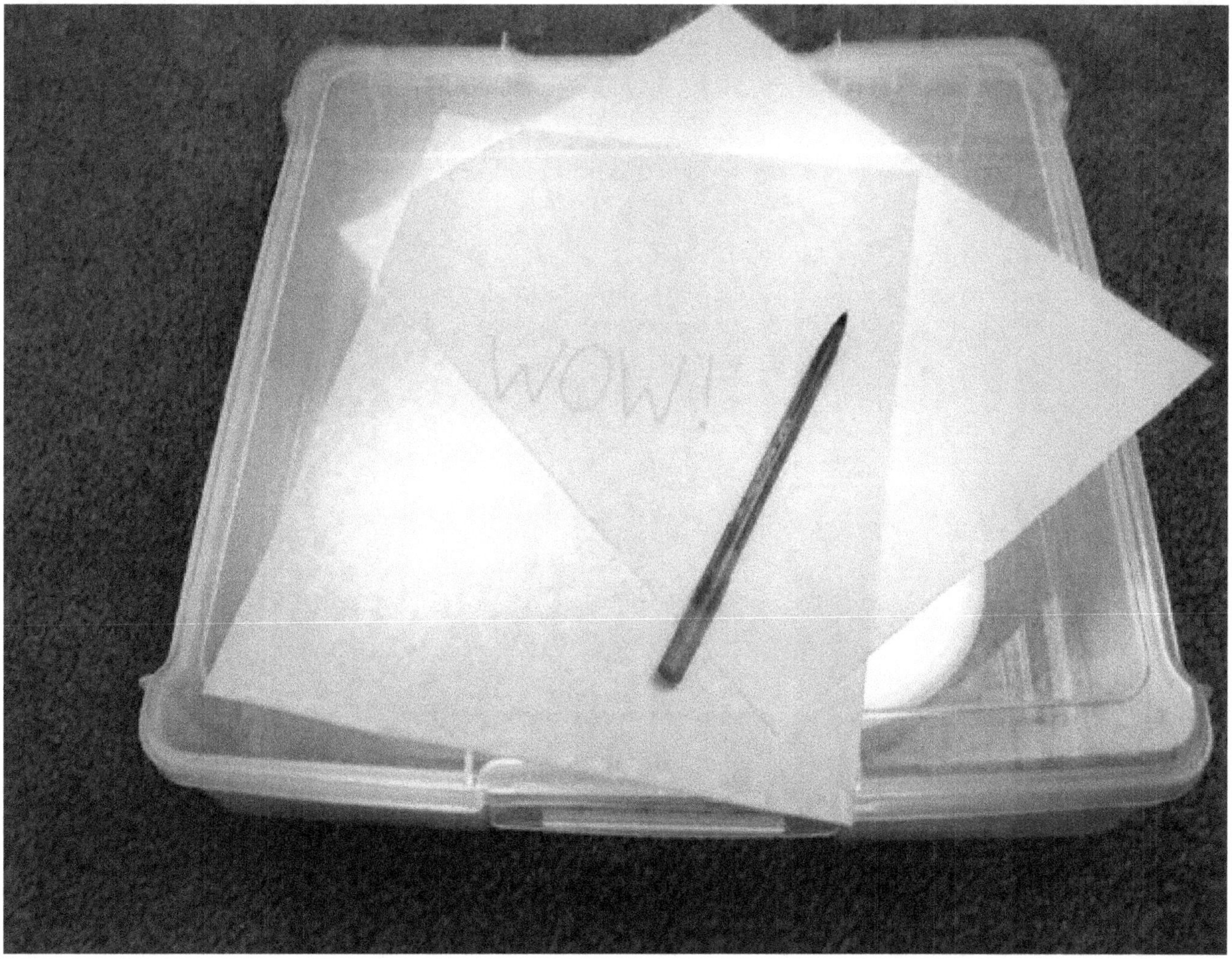

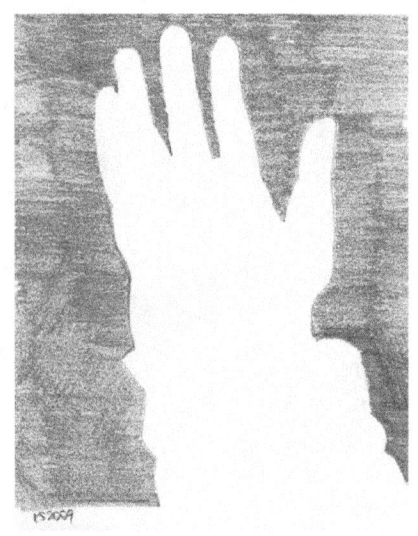
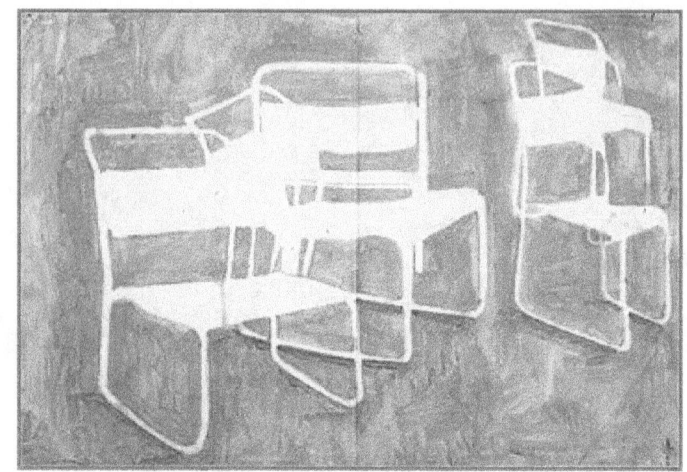
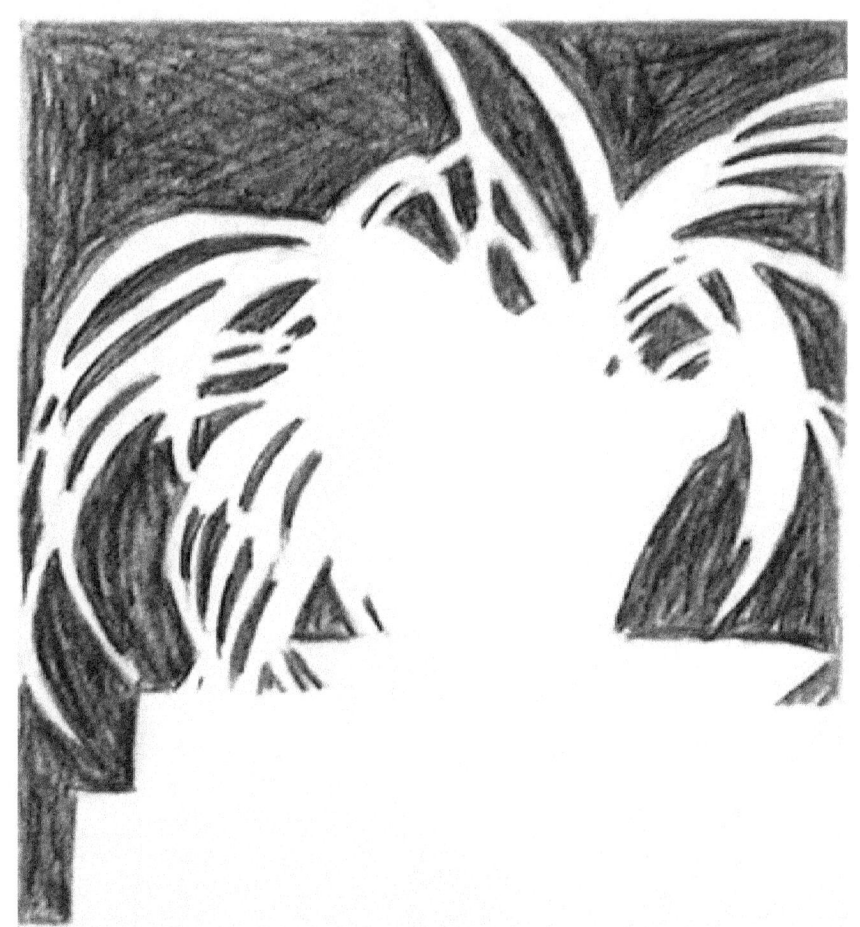

TRY DRAWING EVERYTHING YOU SEE EXCEPT THE OBJECT !

10 FUN STUFF

OK....here we go ! Do these fun, simple exercises and grab some extra paper to add to your "portfolio". Get creative. Not every drawing you do will be...or should be "realistic" Be whimsical, try different styles and techniques. From Da Vinci style to Dr. Suess, you will have more fun...AND surprise yourself if you are flexible. Feel free to write ALL OVER THIS WORKBOOK ! I have left plenty of "doodle" space ! Now go back to the page where you drew all those silly and boring squares, circles and triangles (yes, even the 3D ones and shaded ones and try to turn them into something real...use the examples below or make up your own...HAVE FUN ! Go outside or into another room and find something that is roughly the shape of one of your practise drawings and draw it.
These first few are Jon's:

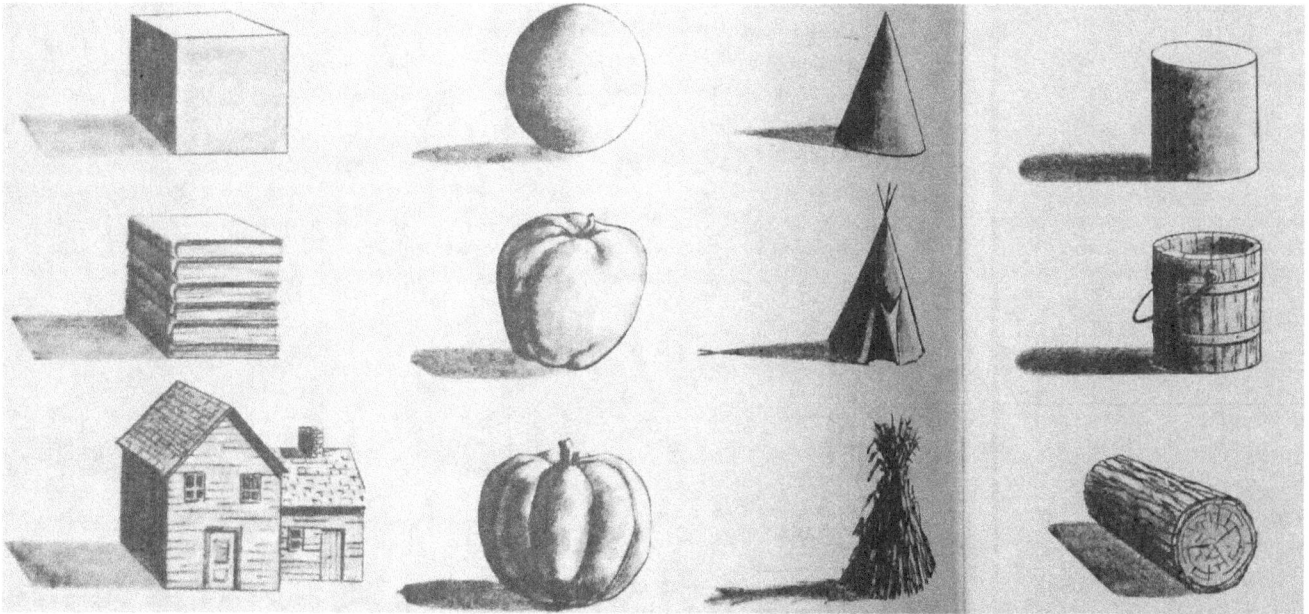

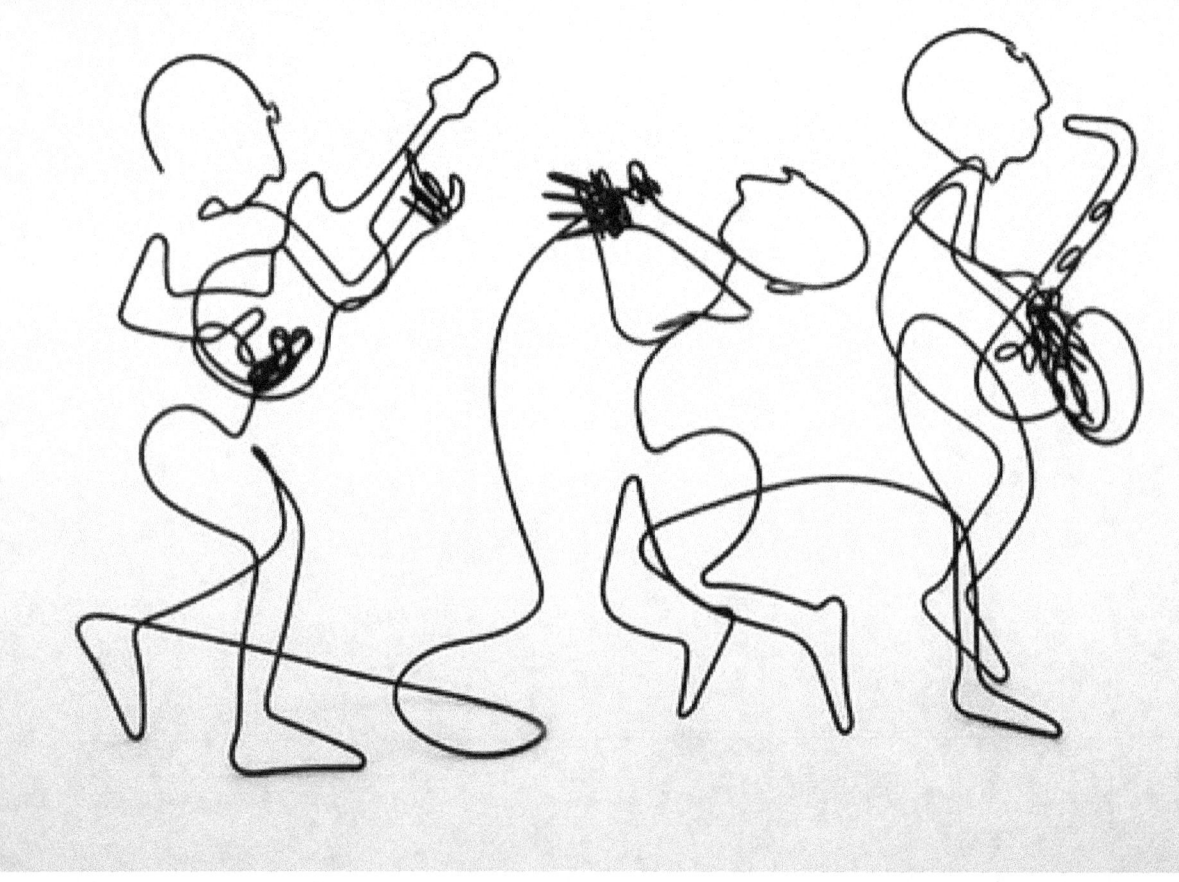

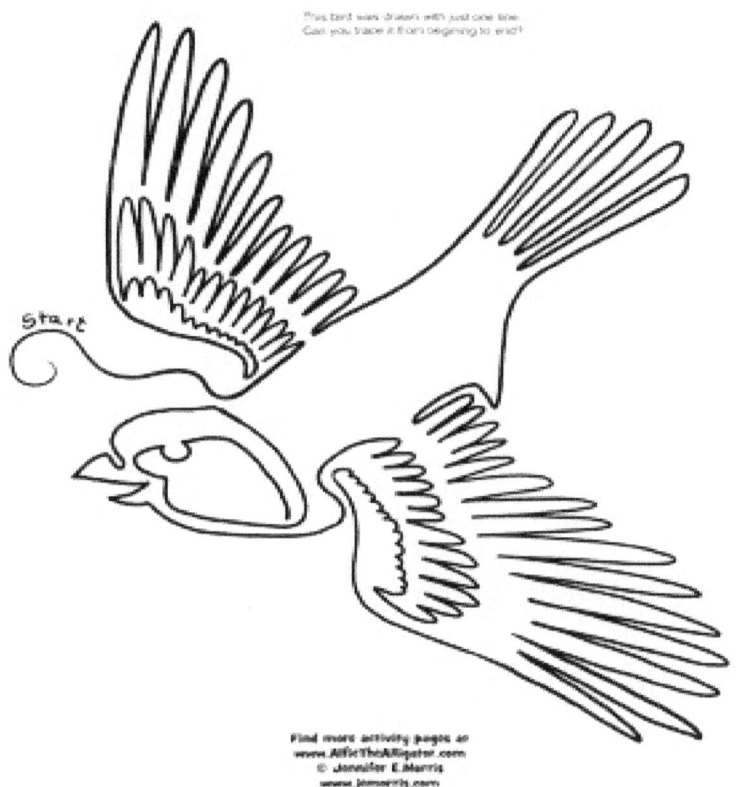

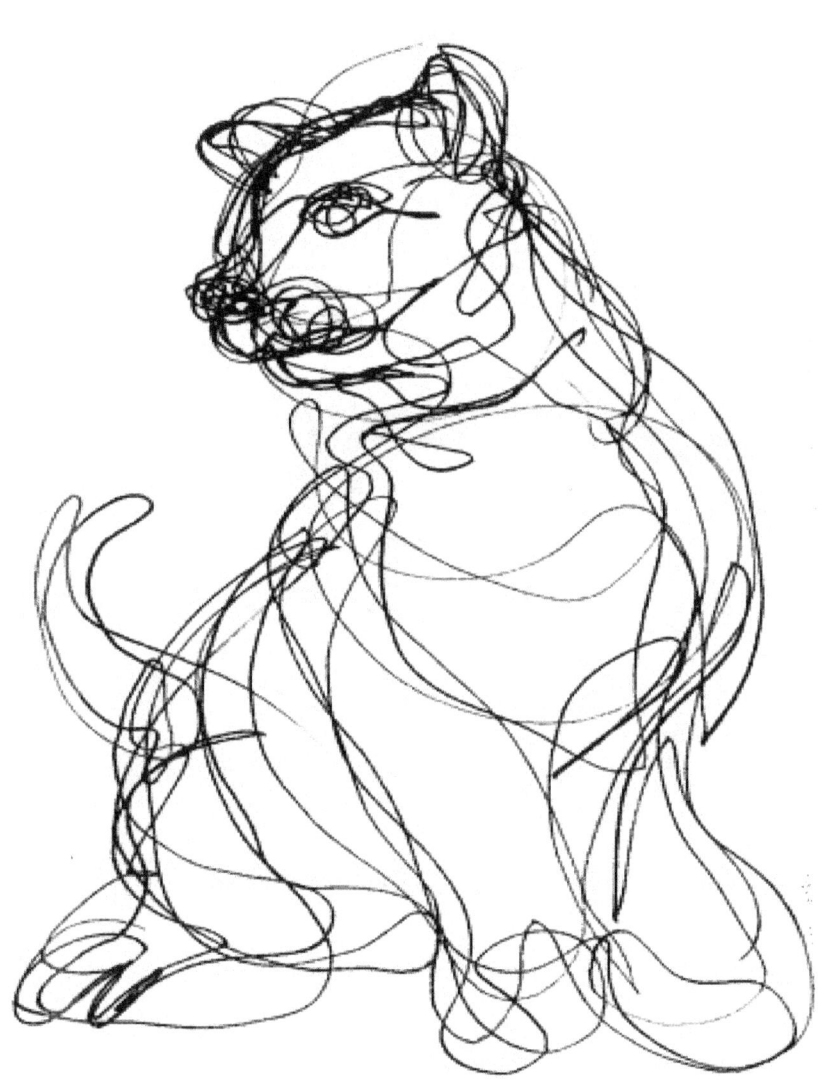

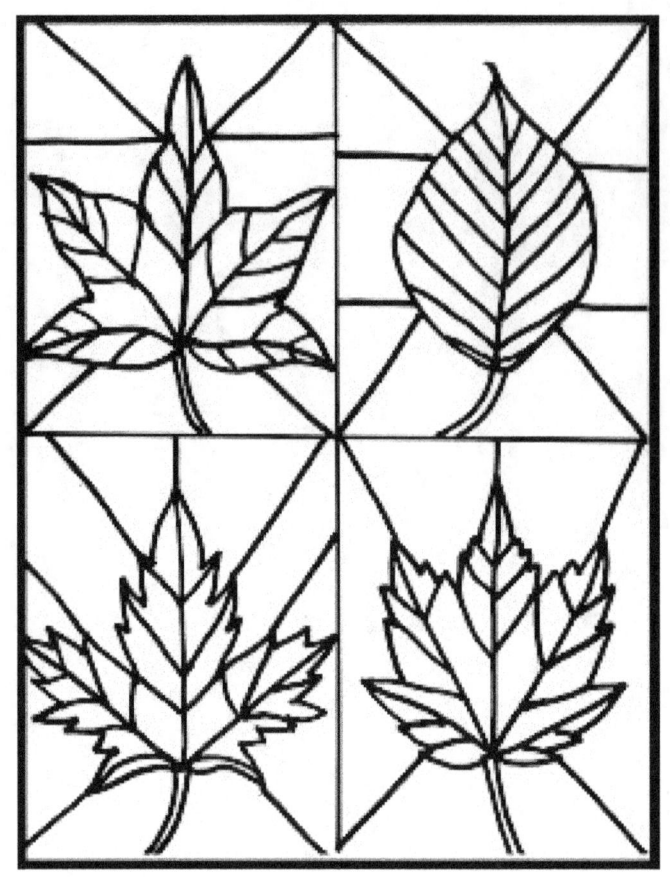

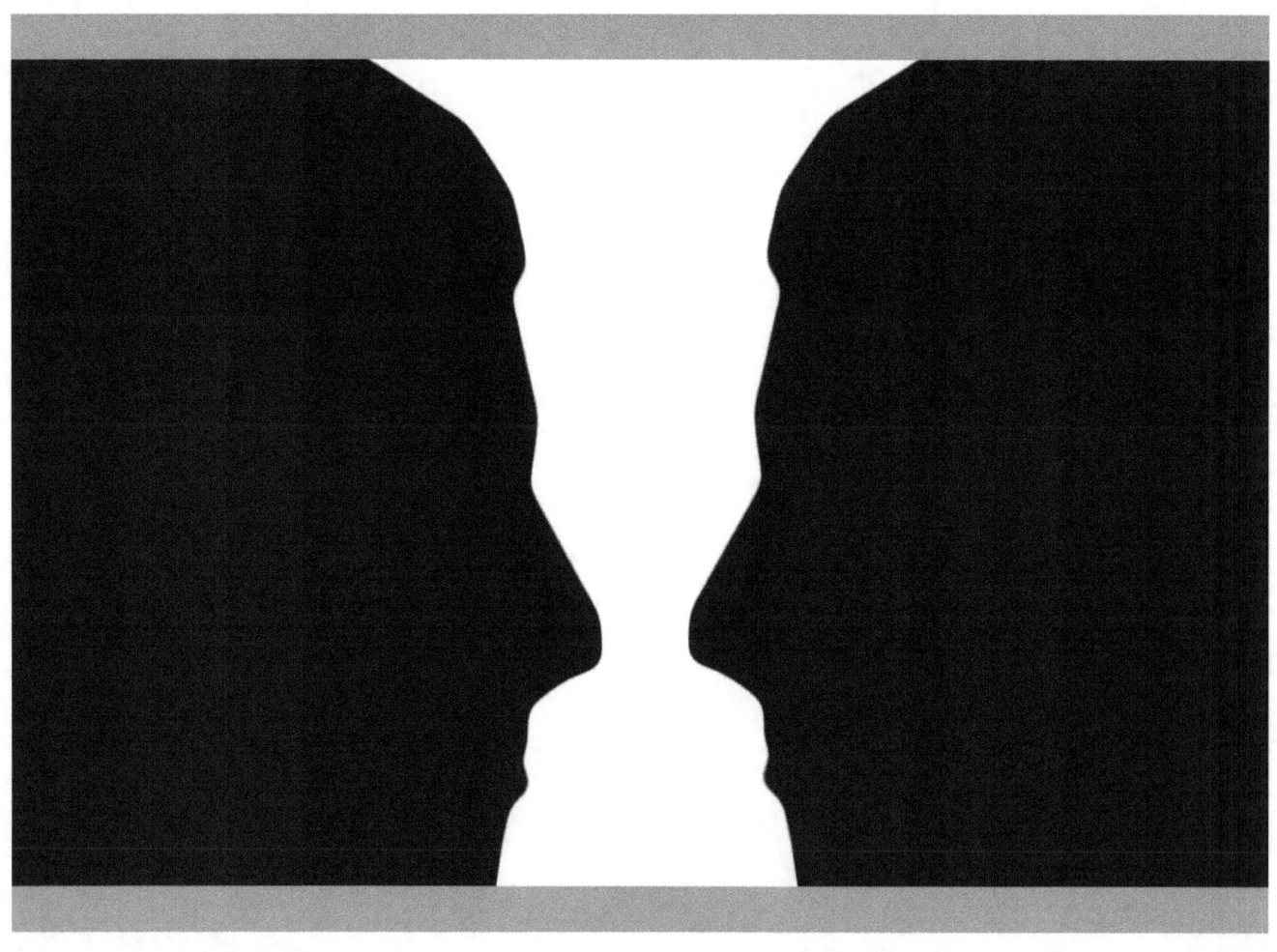

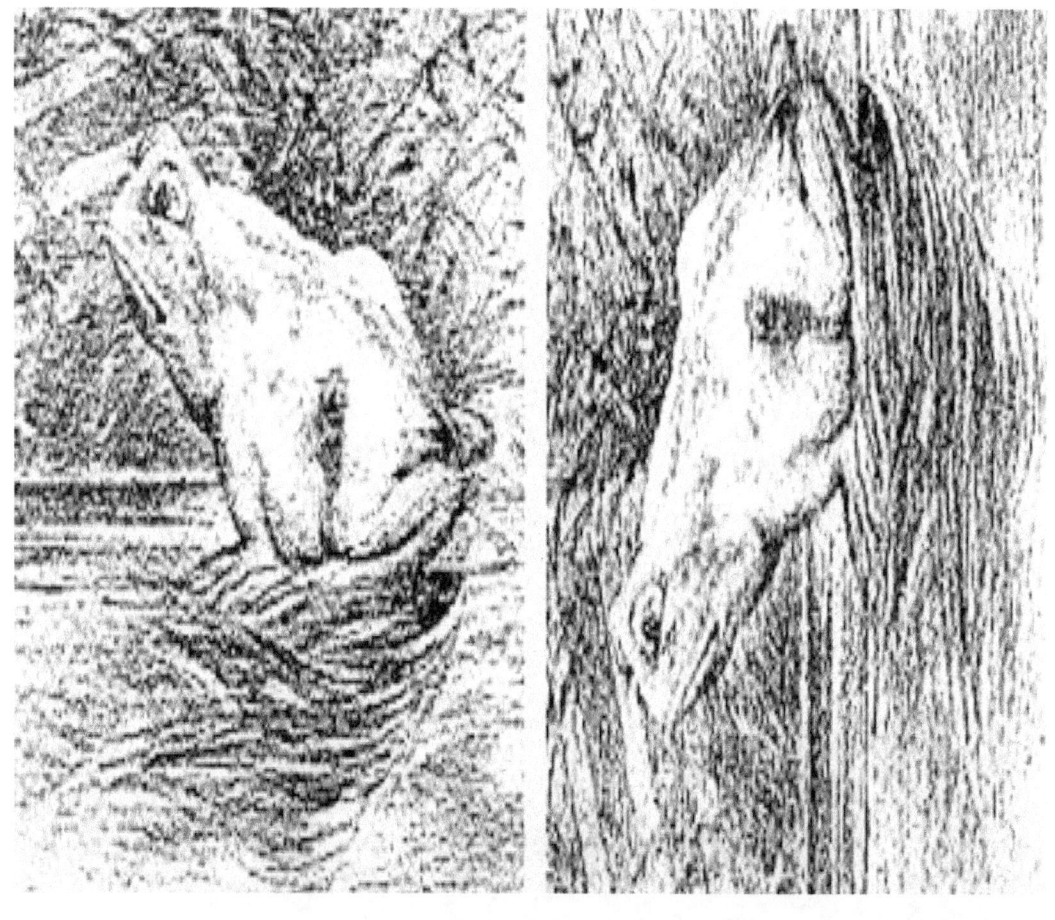

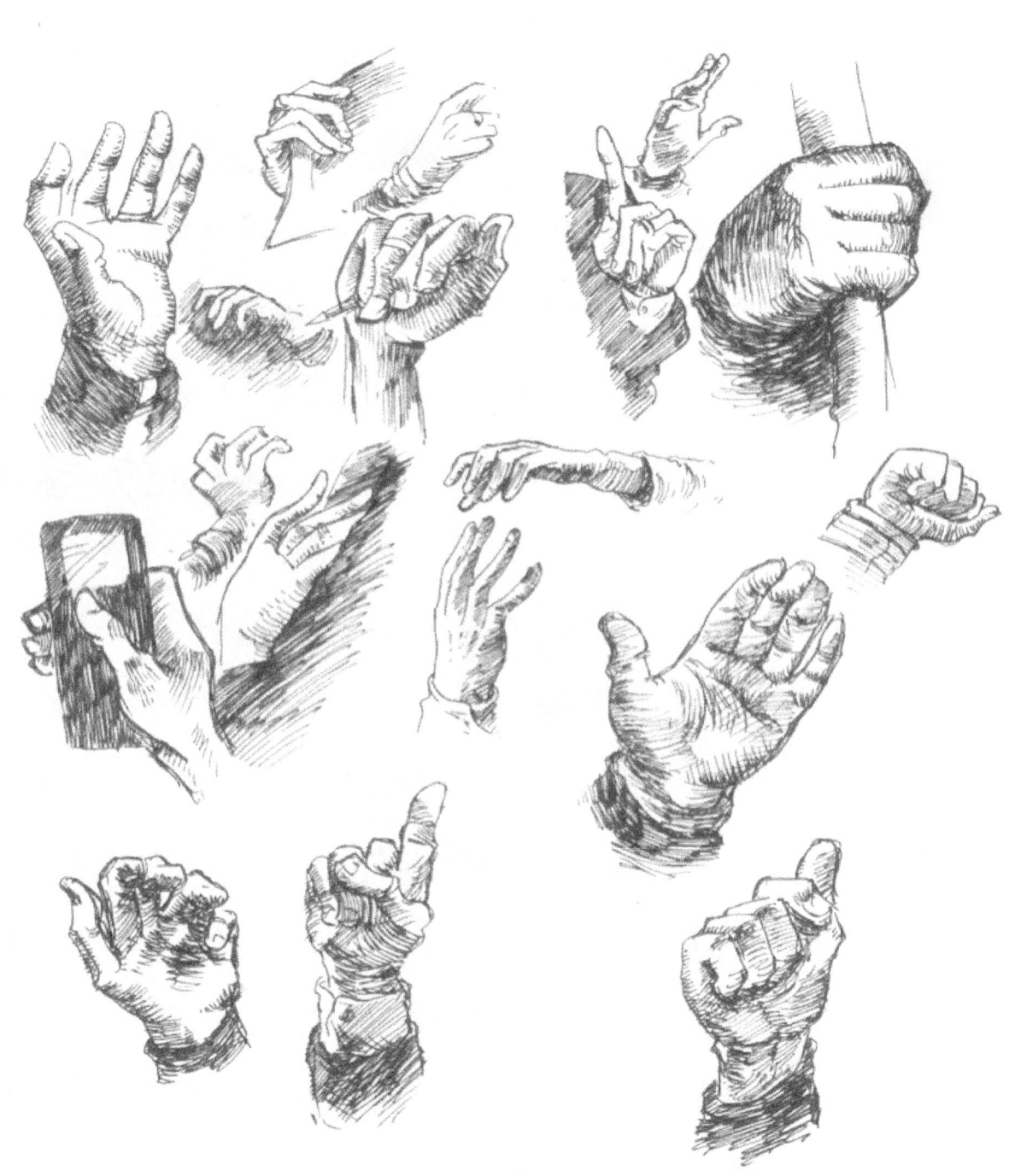

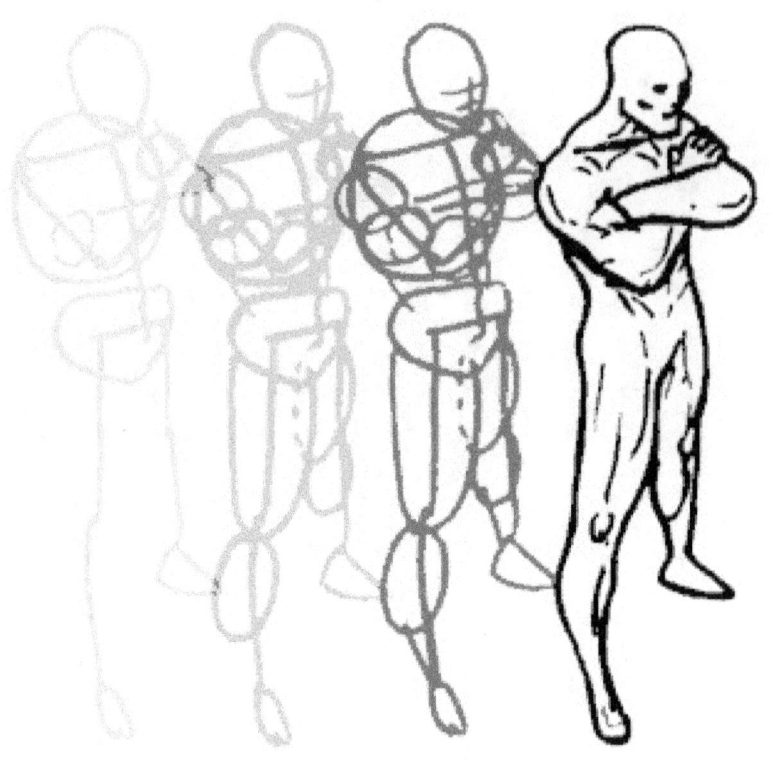

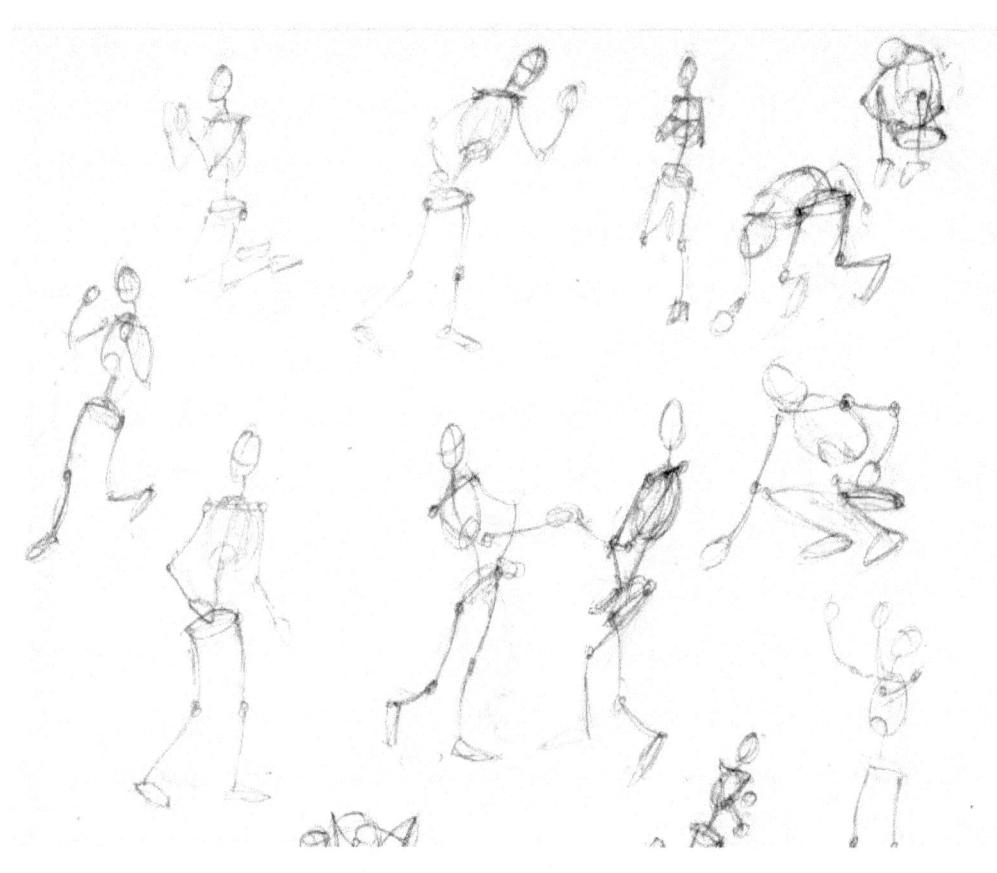

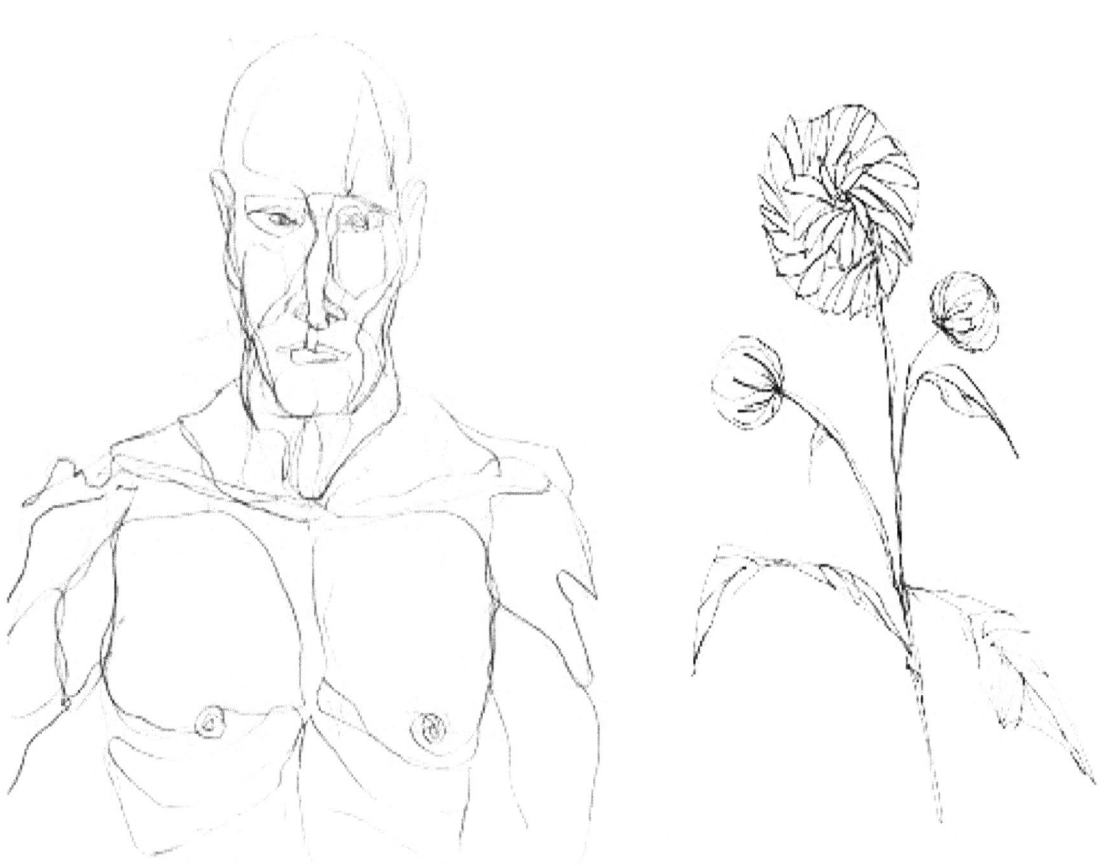

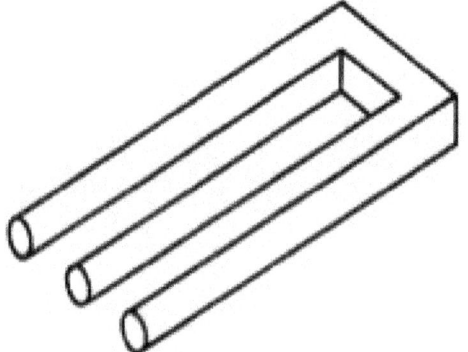

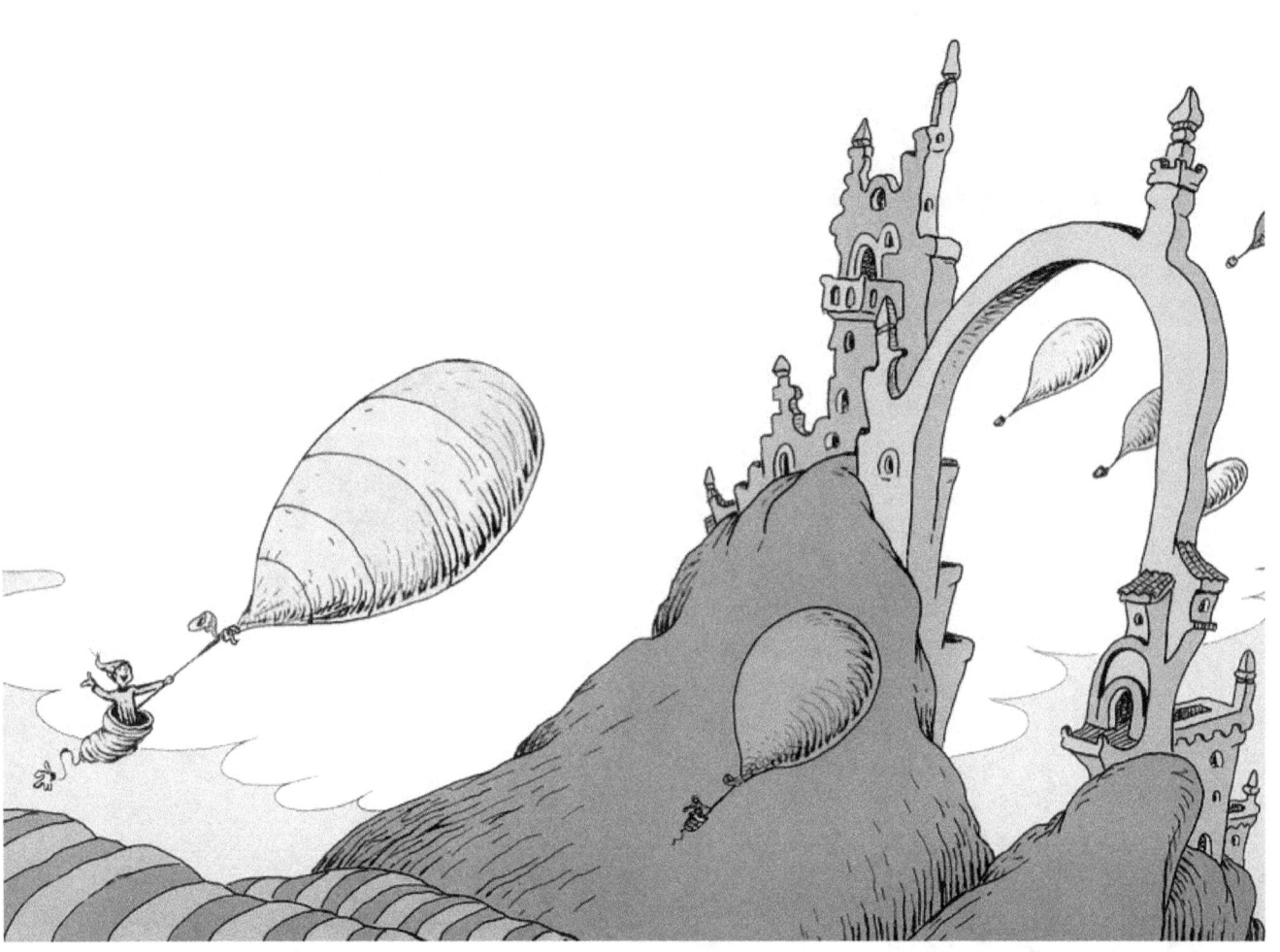

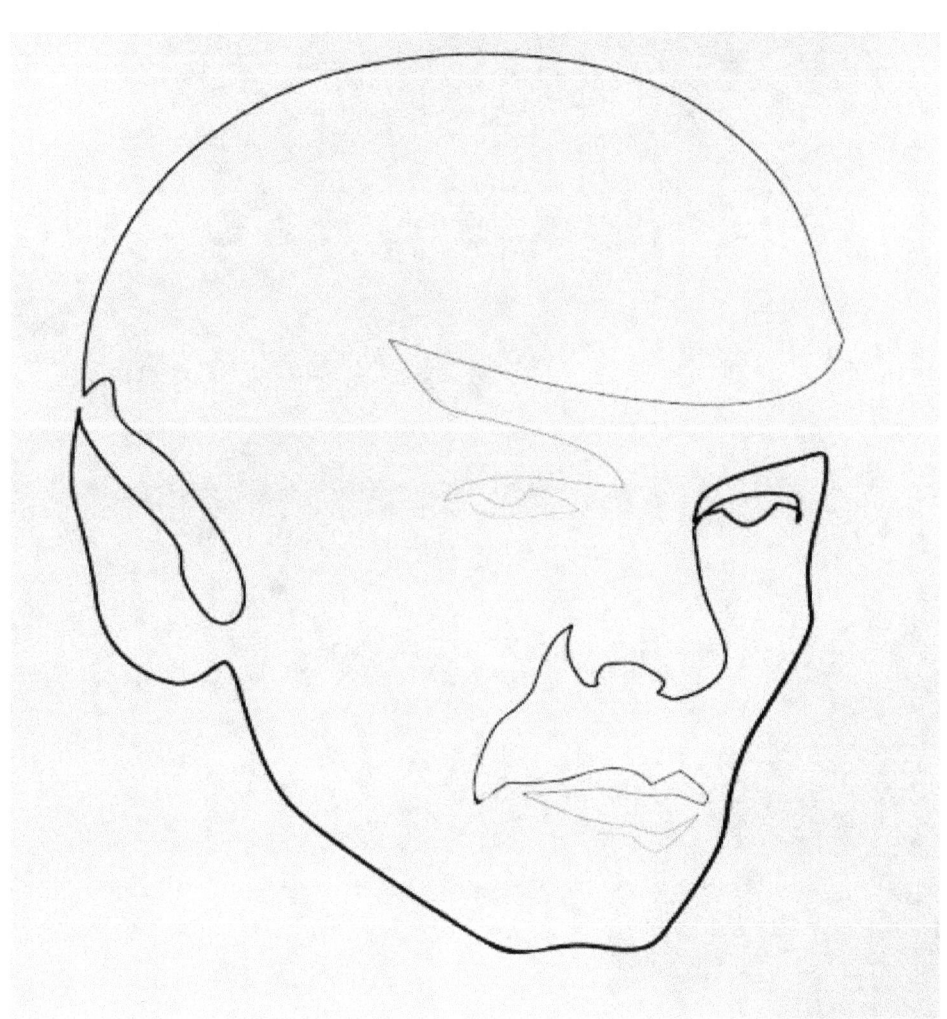

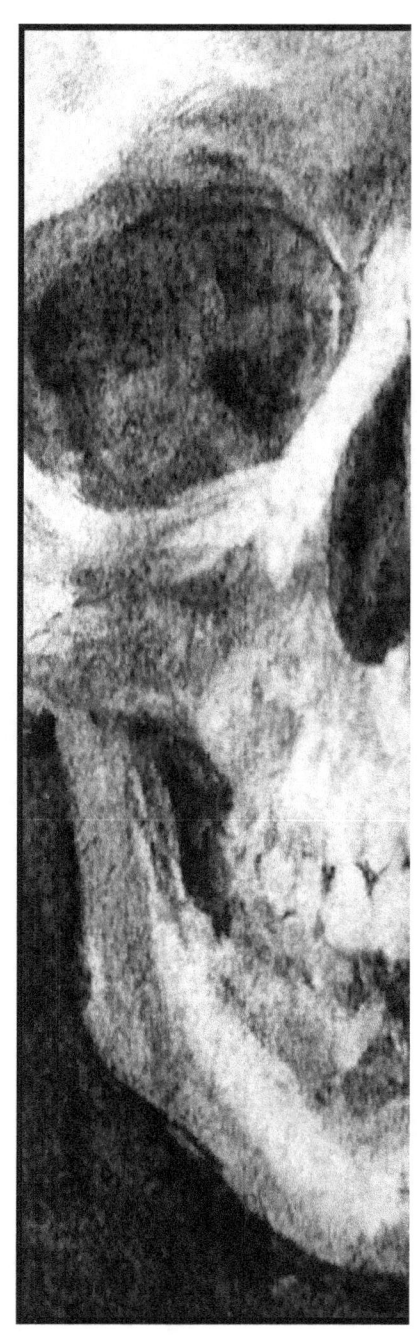

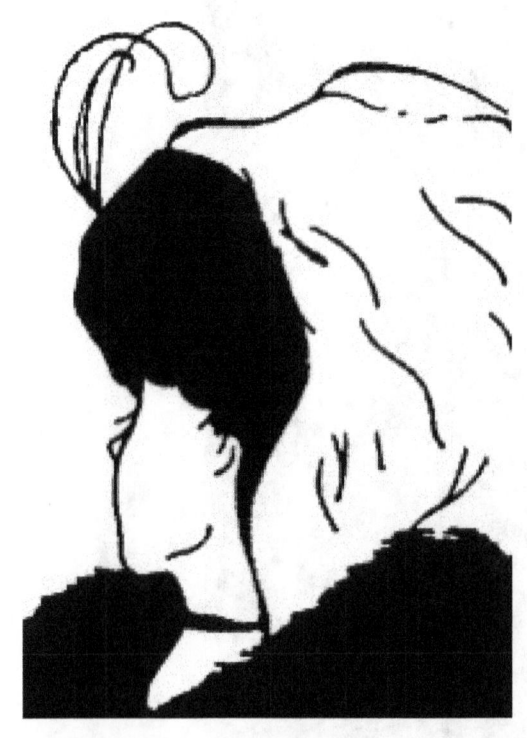

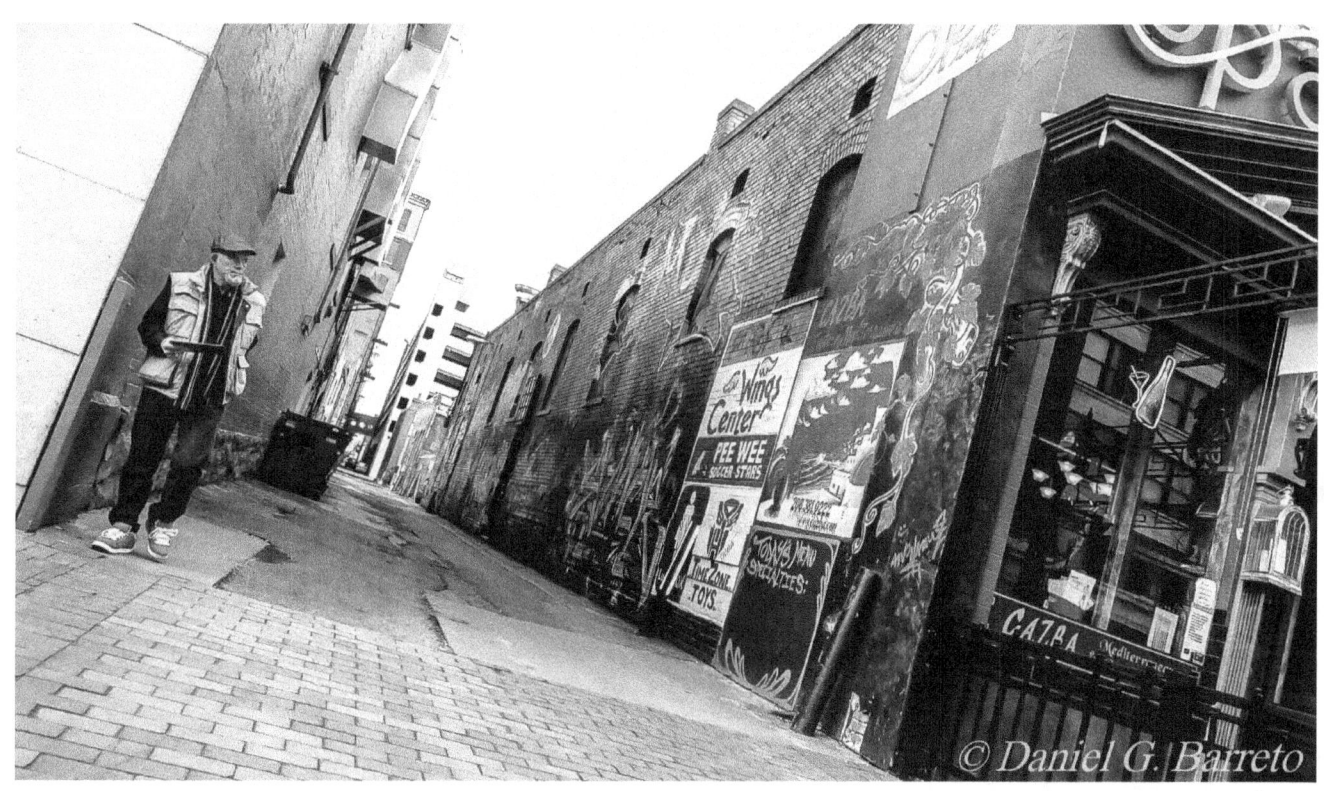

ABOUT THE AUTHOR

Brad L. Johnson has been a writer since 1976 when his first submitted work, a poem, was published by a National Magazine. Since then, he has discovered his "voice" in a wide range of writings from non-fiction to novels, articles, essays and speeches. When he isn't "on the road" with his wife, Linda, they spend their time between a mountaintop in New Mexico and a house near the beach in Baja California. Since 2005 he has published 6 books with 6 more "in the works". You can catch up with him at www.bradljohnson.webs.com.

Note from the author:

" I recently made a trip to Idyllwild, CA, where Jon Gnagy made his home until he passed in 1981. I was fortunate enought to visit the former location of his home and studio, which is now the Mile High Cafe on 243, talk with Bob Smith at the Idyllwild museum who graciously dug through their archives to show me two origianal color drawings by Jon and talk to a few residents and shop-keepers who knew and loved him. This is a great little town that boasts a dog for a mayor, plenty of "hippie shops", natural beauty that is amazing and plenty of great places to see, eat and play."

www.ingramcontent.com/pod-product-compliance
Lightning Source LLC
Chambersburg PA
CBHW080244180526
45167CB00006B/2406